The TROPHY HUNTER

The TROPHY HUNTER

THE *Final* CHRONICLES OF A WEST COAST FISHING GUIDE

David Giblin

FOREWORD BY *Kerriann Cardinal*

Heritage House Publishing Company Ltd.
heritagehouse.ca

Cataloguing information available from Library and Archives Canada
978-1-77203-555-1 (paperback)
978-1-77203-556-8 (e-book)

Edited by Lenore Hietkamp
Proofread by Nandini Thaker
Cover and interior design by Setareh Ashrafologhalai
Cover image by David Giblin

Image on page vi: "Segunda Mujer de Tetaku" (Second Wife of Tetaku), attributed to José Cardero, from the Malaspina expedition, circa 1792. Museo de América, Madrid. Photograph: Gonzalo Cases Ortega.

The interior of this book was produced on 100% post-consumer recycled paper, processed chlorine free, and printed with vegetable-based inks.

Heritage House gratefully acknowledges that the land on which we live and work is within the traditional territories of the lək̓ʷəŋən (Esquimalt and Songhees), Malahat, Pacheedaht, Scia'new, T'Sou-ke, and W̱SÁNEĆ (Pauquachin, Tsartlip, Tsawout, Tseycum) Peoples.

We acknowledge the financial support of the Government of Canada through the Canada Book Fund (CBF) and the Canada Council for the Arts, and the Province of British Columbia through the British Columbia Arts Council and the Book Publishing Tax Credit.

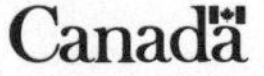

29 28 27 26 25 1 2 3 4 5

Printed in Canada

For the nurses—Kim, Andrea, Jamie, Lana, Deb, and Lisa—as well as the front desk staff—Melanie, Kathy, and Robin—of the Cowichan Community Cancer Clinic. Thank you for taking such kind, wonderful, thoughtful care of me.

Segunda Muger de Tetaku

CONTENTS

FOREWORD

WHEN I FIRST MET David Giblin, it was through his wife, Kimmie. She mentioned he'd been writing stories based on his adventures as a fishing guide, and I was instantly intrigued. I've always had a love for nature and storytelling, a passion inspired by my kookum (Cree for grandmother), who taught me to listen for stories from the land, the water, and the people.

As a Métis theatre artist and documentary filmmaker dedicated to uplifting Indigenous voices and stories, I'm drawn to narratives that are grounded in place, layered with humour, and infused with spirit and bone-deep truth. David's stories embodied all of that—and more.

We spoke often while he was writing this book. David would share snippets—characters he was developing, scenes he was shaping—but what we kept coming back to was the experiences of the Indigenous characters who appear throughout the story. He wanted to honour the time he spent with a fellow Indigenous fishing guide, someone who brought wisdom, laughter, and a completely unique way of seeing the world. That relationship left a mark on David, and it shaped the story in meaningful ways, grounding it in respect, humility, and a deeper sense of connection both on the page and in real life.

Reading the manuscript felt like hopping into the boat with him, going along for every cast, story, and splash. There's something magical in David's storytelling. He writes with the ease of someone who's lived it all—the absurd, the awkward, the quiet, the exhilarating—and still manages to laugh at himself.

Yes, this is a book about fishing. There are rods and reels and lines tangled with possibility. There are clients who think they know everything, and clients who (bless them) definitely do not. There are fish who cooperate, and others who snatch your bait and your dignity like tiny aquatic outlaws. But to say this book is *just* about fishing would miss the point. It's about being human in the wild—and sometimes feeling like the wildest thing in the boat.

David has a particular knack for catching the small moments: the unexpected kindness, the grumbling patience, the endearing weirdness of people you'd never choose to spend time with... and yet find yourself missing when they're gone. His humour shows up like the tide—easy, familiar, and always welcome. And when he lets things get quiet, those moments linger and float along with you.

The Indigenous characters in the book and the water itself act like a compass, grounding the story in something bigger than just hooks and lures. They remind us that these rivers and oceans have stories far older than our own, and that sometimes, the best thing we can do is listen. David doesn't claim to speak *for* Indigenous voices. He makes space for them, respecting their perspectives and honouring their traditions and culture.

So why am I writing this foreword?

Because I believe in stories that come from lived experience. Because I believe laughter is sacred. Because I know what it means to live with a story until you have no choice but to write it down and share it with others. And because David has done exactly that.

If you've ever spent time on the water—or wished you had—this book is for you. If you've ever wondered what really happens on those early-morning fishing trips and if you've ever needed a well-told, good story with a few belly laughs and maybe even a little heart medicine—you're in the right place.

So, pull on a life jacket, grab a thermos of something strong, and climb into the boat. David's waiting to take you on a ride.

KERRIANN CARDINAL

May 2025

one THE TROPHY

THE OLD CAT looked down from his special perch above the cliffs. He was very hungry, not an unusual condition for his kind of predator. The hunger was always there, a driving force throughout his life. In his youth, the encroachment of human settlement on his hunting grounds had forced him to make the perilous, island-hopping journey from Vancouver Island over to the mainland. Driven by his hunger and his instincts, he searched for new territory. The steep, rugged, isolated coastline above Cordero Channel became his home.

Initially, he was disappointed to find a human habitation here, at the south end of the channel where it met the entrance to Bute Inlet. However, the humans seemed happy to stay in that one spot, never venturing up the cliffs and into his territory. Lately, though, he was realizing the benefits that came with such a place.

The cougar was aging and it was getting harder to kill and eat his food. The deer knew he was coming before he could sneak up on them. If he did manage to catch some small rodent by surprise, his teeth couldn't tear into it like they once had. Jumping was more difficult, and sometimes he grunted from the exertion. Perhaps worst of all, his eyes didn't seem to work properly. There was a haze around everything. He had to squint to see what was going on down below.

Down below, a human was burning meat. The cougar didn't need his eyes to tell him that. At least his nose was still working properly. The smell had attracted him from quite some distance away. He had been here before and was never disappointed. The cougar had to admit, these days it was far easier to scavenge here than to hunt.

His hunger had taught him patience. He was content to wait. He knew by now what to expect as day progressed into night. It was not just the anticipation of a feast of barbecued leftovers. He found the behaviour of the humans entertaining. He had been watching from this spot two summers ago when Herbert and his son had lain waste the lodge infrastructure. Of course, the old cat didn't understand the significance of what they were doing, but he did have a cat's instinct for comedy. He was also there last spring, sheltering from a storm, when Nelson went for a ride on the satellite dish. It was a perfect distraction from the inclement weather.

The smoke from the meat wafted past him. The smell of it made him purr. His tail twitched in delightful anticipation. He caught himself drooling. He knew from experience that no one cleaned up at night. The leftovers would sit out until morning, when the humans finally woke. If he waited patiently, the noise would stop and the people would disappear. Then he could sneak down and eat his fill. The old cat put his head down and took a nap.

MEANWHILE, OBLIVIOUS to the eyes that watched from above, Nelson bustled about, getting ready for the party, which he held at Dent Island Lodge every year. Big pieces of meat had been marinating overnight and were now on the grill, cooking slowly. Moose ribs, venison, and salmon all waited for space on the big resort barbecue—probably far more food than people to eat it. However, Nelson had to empty the freezers to make room for the more gentrified tastes of the returning guests.

The new season was about to start. This would be the last gathering of its type for the locals until the summer was over.

WHEN THE BIG CAT awoke, the sky was dark. Noises and enticing scents still rose up the cliff from below. He listened patiently as the noise subsided, the hoots and hollers waning until there were no more.

Still the old cat waited. As hungry as he was, he didn't want any surprises. Finally, he was satisfied; now was the time to move from his perch.

The moon had risen, and he was thankful for it. Even his night vision, once so acute, was beginning to fail him. As he climbed down to the buildings, his mouth watered. He picked his way carefully and quietly along the humans' path to where the burnt meat smells originated.

What he found was beyond his wildest imaginings. Two flat surfaces were filled with the remains of the feast, much of it left untouched—ribs, whole slabs of boneless meat, and fillets of cooked salmon. It was all burnt to some degree, which spoiled the flavour, but he had to admit it was easier for him to eat it. He sidled up to the two tables like a pensioner moving in on a cruise ship buffet.

He had waited so patiently for this moment that he ate more slowly than usual. He licked each bite before he took it in his mouth, savouring the meal and enjoying it thoroughly. The moon illuminated all the tenderest portions. When finally he had his fill, he contemplated moving some of it to a cache for later. He started looking around to see if he had missed any bigger pieces.

As he passed close to the house, he peered into the big picture window that faced over the back deck. It was dark inside and he had to squint, trying to see through the haze of his eyes. The moon came out from behind a small cloud, and it was then he saw something unbelievable. Another cougar was staring back at him!

The old cougar couldn't trust his eyes at first. He blinked and shook his head, trying to focus. Sure enough, there it was, staring back at him. Probably one of those virile, physically fit three-year-olds who think they own the forest. He had dealt with young male cougars before but never one who was so arrogant as to face him directly. The old cougar was outraged and, without thinking, he uttered a deep guttural snarl. The interloper just stood there stubbornly, staring back at him, his lips lifted to snarl back. The old cougar settled in. If this youngster wanted a test of wills, he was ready for him. They began staring each other down.

two THE TROPHY HUNTER

NELSON SLIPPED OUT from under the bed covers and landed, catlike, on the floor. He was attuned to sounds in the middle of the night, no matter how deeply he slept. There was always something making noise. The creak and groan of the docks moving, the shriek of mooring lines—normal sounds that left him sleeping peacefully. This sound was different. It was out of the ordinary. It had pulled him awake like nothing he had ever heard before. It resonated deep inside him, a visceral snarl that touched him at a primal level.

Crouched motionless beside the bed, Nelson struggled to come fully awake. He didn't want to disturb Gilly, who was still sleeping peacefully. Herbert Crane had recently offered him a kind of partnership in the resort, something that made Nelson very happy. He wanted to show Herbert how seriously he took such an offer. It made Nelson even more sensitive to strange noises and things that might be going wrong. He also didn't want Gilly to know how nervous Herbert's offer made him.

He was still slightly drunk from the party the night before. He stood up slowly, then took a couple of steps toward the bedroom door and stopped. He was wearing nothing but a T-shirt. Something about that sound made him feel exposed and vulnerable and acutely aware of his dangling man parts. He reached for the rifle he kept behind the bedroom door, in need of its cold steel reassurance.

Armed, he quietly left the bedroom and walked stealthily into the kitchen. The sound seemed to come from the breakfast nook, a small side room where guests could get coffee and make toast before an early tide. A door led out onto the back deck and the outdoor kitchen. Moonlight spilled in through all the windows and illuminated the small room with an eerie glow.

A slight movement caught his attention. Nelson turned to the counter where the breakfast preparation took place. He found himself looking into the eyes of a cougar, its head wreathed in a strange blue light.

Instinct took over. Nelson clicked off the rifle's safety with his thumb, swung the gun up to his hip, and squeezed the trigger.

The gun bucked violently in his hands. The sound of the blast echoed in the confined space, deafening him.

Something big and metallic hit the back wall, rebounded, and then skidded off the counter. It landed on the floor with a shattering clang.

Ears ringing, Nelson looked down at the carnage, dumbfounded. Time seemed to slow down. The smell of gun smoke filled the air. The bullet had punched through the side of the big eight-slice commercial toaster, the one that always occupied the same spot on the counter. Took it square in the middle. The toaster now lay like a dead animal on the floor, its electrical cord stretched out behind it.

The ringing that enveloped Nelson prevented him from hearing Gilly approach him carefully from behind.

"Nelson?" She stopped a few steps away. She was as dumbfounded as he was. "What did you just do?"

Nelson heard her, but she sounded so very far away. Her words were distorted, slowed down, like a record playing at the wrong speed.

Gilly came up to him gently and put one hand on his shoulder, careful not to startle him. The other hand she laid firmly over Nelson's hand that held the forestock of the gun.

Looking past him, her hands gently calming Nelson, she took in the scene before her.

"Nelson!" She spoke softly, like she was talking to someone in a trance. "Honey, you just shot the toaster!"

Gilly's statement of the obvious roused Nelson back to some kind of awareness.

"I... umm... I thought... I thought it was a cougar," he said, a man trying to remember a dream and put it to words. "... Thought it was going to eat me!"

He looked around, still expecting to see a dead cougar somewhere. All he saw was the commercial toaster on the floor, the bottom crumb tray hanging out like a tongue, toast crumbs spewed like blood splatter. This was a very dead toaster.

"Oh, Nelson, sweetheart, you're not going to get eaten."

Apparently, Gilly had previous experience with half-naked men and random gunfire first thing in the morning. She remained perfectly calm. Her tone of voice was appropriately kind.

"You shot it, all right! Oh boy, you sure did! You shot it really well."

The motherliness of this approach triggered a response from Nelson that took him back to his childhood.

"I don't understand," he said petulantly, trying to will his explanation into reality. "There was a cougar right there."

He pointed to the place the toaster occupied only a few moments before.

"On the counter, Nelson? There isn't enough room on the counter for a cougar. You must have been seeing things."

Gilly, who had been jerked out of a deep sleep by the sound of the gunshot, was now wide awake. The now empty place on the counter was lit by the glow of the moon coming through the window. As she looked over at the window, she began to put it all together. Maybe a cougar had been looking through that window. There had been reports of cougar sightings on this side of the inlet. Perhaps Nelson had seen its face as a reflection in the shiny chrome metal.

Gilly was only too aware that Nelson, a bit tipsy from the night before, was still holding a high-powered hunting rifle.

"Honey, that old toaster isn't going to bother you anymore. That gun must be getting heavy by now," she said in her most soothing tone. She felt his hand on the rifle relax a little. Nelson looked up from the carnage on the floor.

"You give that heavy old gun to me, sweetheart, then maybe we can go and sit down for a minute."

Nelson was beginning to come out of the trance. He let Gilly take the gun gently out of his hands. With the quick deft movements of someone who has had much experience in handling weapons, she put the safety back on, ejected the spent cartridge, leaving the bolt open, then removed the magazine and leaned the rifle against the counter.

three THE FULL-BODY MOUNT

THE OLD COUGAR bent all his will into staring down the interloper. Time stood still as their eyes locked. They both curled their lips into a vicious sneer. The old cat squinted and leaned forward, trying to see through his opponent. The opponent leaned forward. The cougar's lips twitched. His opponent's lips twitched. The cougar knew he was in for the fight of his life.

He had lost track of how long he had been frozen, standing so still. Suddenly, there came a loud noise that startled even his ancient ears. A great ringing crash followed. The old cougar ducked instinctively. After a moment, he carefully raised his head again. The young interloper had vanished. It took a moment for it all to settle in. Then the cougar realized: he was the victor in this test. He had made the young upstart vanish, just like that. He still had it. He was still the feared lord of the woods.

Rustling sounds came from inside the building, and the old cat decided it was time to retire for the night. That sudden noise was sure to arouse the humans. He turned and quietly padded back in the direction he had come from. He was in no hurry. He savoured all that had happened. His belly was full and satisfied, and an important victory over some young upstart was his. He found himself contemplating a certain female that he had lain with in the past. She possessed the most provocative purr. He was more than ready for a visit; it had been too long.

The cougar smiled as he walked away, picking a path toward the old canoe and into the forest. He purred to himself. The idea of what was about to happen, the anticipation, filled his thoughts. His smile widened. His gait quickened. He was overwhelmed with refreshed desire, and his heart pounded in his chest. It was then, in mid-stride and smiling to himself, that his old heart finally gave out.

"HELLO? HERBERT? Yeah, this is Nelson. Nelson. That's right, calling from the resort. Over."

"Hey, Nelson! Good to hear from you. How are things up there in the Canadian wilderness? Uh, over?"

Nelson, still hungover from the night before, really wasn't looking forward to this conversation. He was only too aware he had blown a hole in an expensive kitchen appliance. This wasn't going to help convince Herbert of Nelson's fitness as a business partner. Calling Herbert over the resort radio telephone didn't make it any easier.

"I guess that's what I am calling about. Listen, Herbert, I must tell you about what happened here earlier this morning. I have to replace the toaster—you know, the big commercial one we use in the kitchen. It's going to cost some money. Over."

"Well, if you need a new toaster, just get one. I mean, it's not that big a deal. But what happened to the old one? Over."

"I, um, I shot the old one. Over."

"You what? Over."

"I thought it was a cougar. Over."

"A cougar? You had a cougar get inside the resort? Over."

Herbert shouted to his wife, who must have been in the room with him. "Hey, Nelson's on the phone. A goddamn cougar attacked the resort!"

"Well, no, it wasn't exactly an attack, it was more like an appearance." Nelson didn't want to get into details, but he felt some clarification was necessary. "The cougar wasn't inside the—"

"Goddamn it. You guys are okay, though? You didn't get hurt, I hope. Over."

"No, no, we're okay. Nobody got hurt. Over."

"Somebody needs to find the damn thing. We can't have a dangerous wounded animal around threatening the guests. Over."

"No, it's all taken care of. The cougar is dead. It's no longer a problem. Gilly found it outside down by the Outrigger Canoe Memorial. Over."

"What the hell? She found it. Gilly did what? You mean you shot it inside the resort, then Gilly went out and finished it off? A dangerous wounded animal like that. Damn! She's a hell of a woman, you know."

"No, she didn't finish it off... I mean it was just lying there, and..."

Nelson's voice trailed off. He was knew it was impossible to get Herbert off a certain train of thought once he had gotten started. Like a boulder gathering momentum, Herbert continued to relay his own version of events to his wife.

"Do you believe it? Those two fought off a goddamn cougar attacking the resort," Herbert grandly announced beyond the receiver. "What's that? I know, they're doing one hell of a job up there. Can you imagine? It's just the two of them up there alone against the goddamn wilderness."

"So, hey," said Herbert, returning to Nelson. "Where is the cougar now? Over."

"We haven't moved it yet. It's lying by the outrigger canoe. It looks like it just dropped in mid-stride—"

"Tell you what," Herbert interjected once more. "Clean out the big freezer—you know the one. Then you wrap that cat up in some garbage bags or something and freeze it. I'll fly up in a day or two and pick him up. I know a guy down here in Seattle. One of them taxidermists who could do what they call a full-body mount. It's not just the head but the whole cat—you know, rearing up on its hind legs and snarling, looking really fierce! We could put that right in the main room. It would be a hell of a thing."

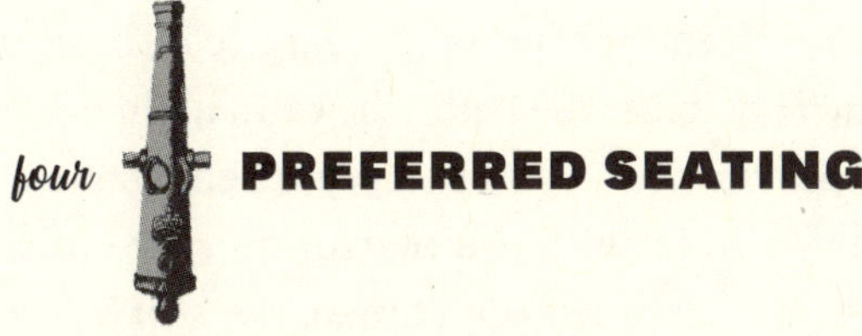

four PREFERRED SEATING

I REACHED STUART Island a little earlier than normal and had the cabin to myself for a few days. I had made it to Nelson's Start of the Year Party for the first time.

There were many stories about these legendary gatherings, most of them regarding the food and beverages that appeared for the occasion. Food was always more plentiful than could possibly be eaten in a single night. Along with the last of the frozen moose meat and deer appeared canned, smoked salmon, fresh-caught codfish, and clams.

Nelson had fired up the big lodge barbecue, with rotisseries over the grills slow-roasting various meats. The codfish was in clay bakers atop layers of rock salt and pine needles. Nelson had made his favourite sausage, laying it out on the grill too.

People brought seasonal food they foraged in the woods—young shoots of fiddlehead ferns and even shoots of young skunk cabbage, which, despite its rather unfortunate name, was delicious. To wash it all down, a dark red, almost black, wine made from local blackberries and a sparkling wine made from rose hips.

And Carl always sent up a bag of his best weed, whether he himself could attend or not.

I wasn't around for the gunfire. I was back at the cabin in Big Bay on Stuart Island, sleeping peacefully. All of us had left around two in the morning to make it home through the rapids at the slack tide. Some of the resort staff returned to various places elsewhere in Big Bay, while a large contingent made the run all the way to Read Island. The calm night with a full moon made the trip after such a party quite enjoyable.

Word of Nelson's run-in with the toaster quickly circulated through the usual channels. Of course, the story was accompanied by a mixture of fact and fiction.

I heard all about it from Troutbreath. I stopped in at the gas dock the next day to fill my tanks and pick up my first batch of herring for the year.

"Yeah, Nelson was by here earlier," said Troutbreath, as he concluded the story. "I tried to convince him they should mount the toaster and display it in the main room too, but I think it's a sensitive subject for him."

"Still too soon?"

"I should have maybe waited a couple of days."

As usual, Troutbreath also gave me an update and useful information on some of the new guides. He wanted to talk to someone about one of them in particular.

"His name is Lawrence. He's from up-coast. I may have gotten myself in trouble, though," Troutbreath said.

"What have you done this time?" I asked tentatively, not really wanting to know.

"You know me, I can't help spreading spurious lies and rumours. See those two guys waiting on the gas dock to go fishing? I may have led them to believe something about their guide, Lawrence, that isn't necessarily true." Troutbreath shrugged and gave me that sheepish grin of his. Then he saw someone coming down from the resort, still some distance away. "Here comes Lawrence now. Go fill some gas tanks."

I couldn't help but be curious. Taking Troutbreath's suggestion, I walked casually back to my gas tanks that stood on the dock near the guests. Both men were adorned with black windbreakers that said "Tydesco Chemical." I started up one of the pumps and began filling my tanks.

As the gas flowed, I listened in on the conversation between the two men. Apparently, they were impatiently waiting to go fishing with a "Wild Indian." No doubt someone—Troutbreath—had planted a seed.

The two became embroiled in a convoluted discussion about who had the better light cavalry, the Comanches or the Mongols. Not that light cavalry was much use in the mountains around Big Bay. Their conversation was not unlike many others I, as a seasoned guide, have had to sit through in my boat.

My first tank was full. I looked back to see Lawrence still making his way over. He was one of the rookie guides, the supposed "Wild Indian" who was the subject of the guests' conversation. He was in no hurry. His slow, rolling gait down the dock suggested he had long experience walking on things that moved underfoot. He stopped beside a guide boat tied off in Troutbreath's usual spot.

He and Troutbreath must have had a special relationship of some kind if Troutbreath let him tie up his boat at the gas dock. That was unheard of. It was a privilege usually reserved for Lucky Petersen, Big Jake, or one or two other very senior guides. The rookies' boats were all squashed together, far from the gas and the herring boxes. It had proven to be a wise policy: keeping them where they could have as little interaction with the guests as possible. Guest pick-up and drop-off was carefully organized. It was one of the ways Troutbreath exercised his control.

As the new guide reached the boat, the two guests stood up straight and put their shoulders back. They stuffed their hands in the pockets of their windbreakers, scuffed their boots on the dock, and shifted, leaning back, like they might spit into the water at any moment. Despite their windbreakers, they might have been extras in a bad western.

Lawrence raised his eyebrows and looked at the two. "You fellows looking to go fishing?" he asked.

He smiled broadly, clearly amused at something. I recalled that Troutbreath had alluded to some exaggeration. It seemed to have made Lawrence enjoy the situation.

"My name is Lawrence. I guess you'll be going out with me."

"So, uh… Lawrence?" began one of the men, who looked Lawrence over carefully. The question in his voice implied that "Lawrence" wasn't exactly the name the man was expecting. "Yeah, uh," he continued, "I guess you're the guy we've been waiting for."

The guest looked a little awkward now. It became clear why with the next question he asked. I listened in stunned silence.

"So, what are you—Cheyenne, Sioux, a Pawnee, maybe—maybe an Arapaho?

"Oh, no," said Lawrence. He cleared his throat, the low chuckle of a raven emerging gently. "I'm a Bella Coola."

I noticed that, for some reason, Lawrence deliberately used the older name that was slowly being phased out. The look of consternation on the faces of the two guests was telling. A Bella Coola? Somehow, this Lawrence guy didn't quite live up to what they were expecting.

Lawrence, still smiling broadly, helped the sulking guests into his boat.

AS THEY MOTORED AWAY from the dock, Troutbreath came up beside me. "You believe those two chuckleheads? They gave me money to go fishing with Lawrence. They think he's a 'Wild Indian'!"

I threw Troutbreath my best side-eye.

"You made them pay money to go fishing with a 'Wild Indian'? Seriously?"

"Oh yes, and they paid quite handsomely too. They outbid two other guys."

"What do you mean, 'outbid'?"

"Oh yeah, I left that part out. We held an auction," Troutbreath said blandly.

"You held an auction? What? I don't understand. What did you auction?"

"We auctioned off the privilege of going fishing with Lawrence."

"You auctioned off a seat in Lawrence's boat? He's a first-year rookie guide!"

I was having a hard time wrapping my head around it all.

"Sure, he's a first-year rookie, but more important is that he's a 'Wild Indian,'" said Troutbreath, frowning a little, then smiling ruefully. "Several people wanted the opportunity to go fishing with him. Think of it as using the free market to establish a fee for preferred seating."

"I hope you intend to split that 'fee' with Lawrence."

"Split it with him?" Troutbreath seemed genuinely hurt. "He came up with the idea in the first place! I didn't think we could find anyone who was... who was that—well, you know, who would do it. I never expected to be holding a damn auction."

From the pained expression on his face, I suspected Troutbreath had also lost something, maybe money, from this outcome. Perhaps it explained how a rookie got to leave his boat so conveniently at the gas dock. As we talked about the new guide, I heard something in Troutbreath's voice that had never been there before, at least as far as talk about a rookie was concerned: I heard respect.

Troutbreath and I got down to business. There were always people to take out fishing on a weekend, but being successful as an independent guide meant finding work in the middle of the week. To make that happen, you needed to get hired on with the steady boat traffic. The Brelands were back again, but Troutbreath had another customer for not just me but Vop and a couple of the other guides as well.

"I got a call from a boat that's never been here before. It's called *Texas Tea*. The owner must be into oil or something. I mean, he's taken his boat's name from *The Beverly Hillbillies* theme song. I have no idea whether that's significant or not. Anyway, they're coming up in a couple of days with the boat, just to check things out, maybe do some exploring. You interested?"

Of course I was interested in any ongoing work with the yachting crowd, but I was also a little curious. It was hard to stop visions from *The Beverly Hillbillies* television show coming to mind.

"Well, yeah, I'm interested. I'll make a note in my calendar."

"When are you expecting to see Vop?"

This was a more difficult question. Vop was in town picking up a brand-new motor from the dealers. After his now internationally famous flying experience a couple of summers ago, Vop had an aversion to floatplanes. According to Vop, he wasn't afraid of flying. It was all about preserving his decals. He didn't want to fly his new motor in because the lettering decals on his old one had been scratched during the plane's bumpy landing. That was the reason he was still in Campbell River. He was waiting to hook up with a freight boat heading to the island. The captain had assured him his new motor would arrive safely and unblemished. Vop's time of arrival was dependant on that captain's schedule.

"I expect to see Vop today or tomorrow. He's coming up by boat."

I didn't want to explain the whole situation and cause unnecessary concern. I waited for Troutbreath's reply. I knew Troutbreath well enough by now, and there was always going to be one more thing.

"Oh, one more thing, before I forget. So, you won the Stuart Island Community Salmon Derby last summer. Kind of a rookie mistake, if you want my opinion. You realize that means Old Man Lynwood wants to reserve you."

Just hearing Old Man Lynwood's name was enough to sink a guide's heart into a maelstrom of despair. Troutbreath was aware of this and had developed a strategy to deal with our anxiety.

"He is willing to pay you twice the going rate for this summer's Derby Day!"

"What does he want to go out with me for? It wasn't like I did it on purpose. There's no guarantee I could repeat that sort of a catch. Especially on Derby Day, and we all know how much he wants to win it."

It was an honest question. I had never gone out with Old Man Lynwood. Throughout the season, he usually went out with Lucky Petersen, if he used a guide at all. However,

Lynwood's Derby Day tradition was always to book the previous summer's derby winner. But derby winner guides were trying to win, and my win had been pure luck.

"Lucky Petersen had him in first place last year until I came in with that slab. Old Man Lynwood would still be much better off with Lucky Petersen."

Sure, Lucky Petersen had some seriously mixed feelings about losing at the last minute last summer. While he might have been counting on the incredibly large tip that would come with such a feat, winning would have also meant that, according to tradition, he would have to take Old Man Lynwood out for this year's derby. Most of the guests were just there for the day's fun and excitement, so the depth of Lucky Petersen's relief made you wonder. How bad could time in a guide boat with the Old Man really be?

Unfortunately, it seemed Troutbreath was determined I would have the chance to find out for myself.

"You can see the Old Man's point. I weighed that slab and you smoked everybody! You beat Lucky's fish by almost twice as much." Troutbreath folded his arms and looked at me. It was a simple statement of fact: my fish was so big that I must know what I was doing.

"Well, maybe, but..."

In the moment, I couldn't really find a way to deny it.

"So, is that a yes?"

In the end, it wasn't the extra money for my hours, or some extravagant tip. Even the idea of being the toast of the Wheelhouse Pub for putting all the guides out of their misery—by putting Old Man Lynwood out of his—wasn't what made me agree. I just needed to see the guy in action for myself.

"Yeah, I guess so." I let out a big sigh. "Sign me up."

"Try not to sound so enthusiastic," said Troutbreath.

five GREASE

LATER THAT NIGHT, as the guides ate dinner, Troutbreath, with great ceremony, pulled a gallon jug out of a bag and set it in the middle of the table. It was one of those clear glass wine jugs with a little handle you could put your forefinger through.

It still had a label on it, announcing "Kelowna Royal Red."

However, the jug contained a deep amber liquid that, even with the top on, gave off a distinctive aroma that was not from wine.

"Listen up, everyone!" Troutbreath called the table full of guides to some semblance of order.

"I have some important news. You guys have benefitted before from things like the Reserve Box and our mutual wine cellar. Our concerted efforts to help errant boaters has even brought us caviar to go along with the wine. It all helps to make life here that much more enjoyable, doesn't it?"

There was a general murmur of agreement. The returning guides were fully in favour of Troutbreath's system. Even the new rookies had already sampled the wine and the caviar.

"So, not only does my latest acquisition add to that enjoyment, but it can also really make a difference to your overall physical health, living and working as we do." He gently laid his hand on the jug. His gesture suggested that the contents were a rare and special treasure. “It took some bartering with Lawrence here”—Troutbreath nodded toward Lawrence, who was sitting quietly, taking it all in—“but he has agreed to keep us in a steady supply of this.”

“What is it?” one of the guides in the audience yelled out.

“Looks like used crankcase oil,” another offered helpfully.

One of the more practically minded guides asked, “What did your latest acquisition cost us exactly?”

Troutbreath recognized the practicality. “We are going to be sending all the caviar we get north. While Lawrence has arranged to send this south, to us.”

“You did what with our caviar?”

The question from the table at large was met by another murmur of concern from the rest of the guides.

“Hold on, hold on, let me finish. I mean, to begin with, you guys didn’t even know what caviar was when you first started here.”

He gave the jug a gentle spin.

“You need to know what you are looking at here.”

He picked up the bottle and presented it like a sommelier presenting a fine wine. “This is a whole gallon of eulachon oil, usually just called ‘grease.’”

Troutbreath’s revelation was met with complete silence. The puffed-up sommelier deflated a little.

“You guys must know what grease is?” His voice rose in disbelief. “Seriously?”

“You traded away all the caviar?” said a voice from the far table. Troutbreath could feel the room turning against him.

“We kind of liked the caviar!” someone else added, a sentiment that caused a ripple of agreement to circulate around the room.

"Well, caviar might make you feel like some kind of food connoisseur, but trust me, grease is actually good for you." As soon as he said it, Troutbreath knew it wasn't a winning argument.

"You're not my grandmother!" said one guide.

"I had to take cod liver oil when I was a kid and I hated it," shared another.

That's when Big Jake cleared his throat. A hush fell over the dining room. Big Jake could be quite friendly, and he was noticeably polite to the guests; he was even known to be tolerant of the occasional FBI investigation. When it came to the guides, however—well, he was the head guide. Nobody was allowed to forget that.

Big Jake looked down the table. "You shrubs should pay attention to what Troutbreath is trying to tell you. You might learn something. Grease is far better than those fancy fish eggs you guys like to shovel down."

"What do you know about it?"

The question came from some rookie who still had much to learn.

Big Jake reached down inside his fishing sweater and pulled out a small vial. It hung around his neck on a lanyard made from a leather shoelace. He pulled the lanyard over his head and put the vial onto the table next to the wine jug. The glass met the metal table with a sharp click. The small sound seemed to fill the dining room, emphasizing what Big Jake said next.

"Not that any of you ever notice or think about it at all, but I'm here before any of you stragglers show up for the summer. I get the docks ready and put all the boats back into the water. I take some of the early keeners, like Old Man Lynwood, out fishing. When you guys finally do get here, I train all the newcomers, so they don't die in a whirlpool. Then, at the end of the season, long after you scurry back to wherever you came from, I'm still out on the water. Out fishing with Old Man Lynwood. In between pulling the boats out and all the other stuff that happens around here to get ready for winter."

The room was spellbound, watching closely as he then raised his left hand.

"This hand should be crippled by now, after all the time it spends catching herring in my bait tank or being out there on the docks in a blowing gale. The contents of that vial are why I can still move my fingers. That's eulachon oil in that vial." He held up the vial so it could catch the light. Even the greenest rookie in the room was struck by the moment.

"My grandmother"—and here Big Jake drew out the word "grandmother"—"sends me packages and makes sure this little vial is always full. If any of you ever bothered to ask, I could tell you she is Indigenous and knows all about 'grease.' Now, you can mock Troutbreath—he is kind of pompous sometimes. If you are tired of life, you can mock me too. But you shrubs need to show some respect for the people who were here thousands of years before any of us. They might know a few things about surviving in this part of the world."

There was a long silence. Nobody had ever heard Big Jake make a speech like that. Even Troutbreath was quiet and a little awestruck. A couple of people reached out to touch the jug and look more closely at the label, as if there were some further information there, important information they hadn't noticed.

"So, what are we supposed to do with this grease stuff?" asked one of them.

"You eat it," said Troutbreath, his enthusiasm renewed. "You can use it like a dip or pour it over fish or potatoes. It's good with smoked clams—"

"How do you use it, Jake?" Troutbreath was cut off by someone bold enough to ask. There was a distinct possibility here. If Big Jake was wearing a vial full of grease around his neck, taking it with him into the fishing holes, he might be using it as something more than just a condiment.

Jake looked at them from under the peak of his ball cap.

"There are some things you shrubs need to figure out for yourselves. I'm not telling you all my secrets."

With that, Big Jake picked up the vial and slipped it back around his neck. It disappeared into his fishing sweater once again. He pulled his cap down over his eyes and slumped back into his chair at the head of the table. As far as he was concerned, that was the end of the discussion.

six THE ROLLER SKATE STORY

THE MID-WEEK WORK from the *Texas Tea* was a good start to the summer, but I still had to make the regular rounds with my bookings calendar to see who needed another guide. One of my usual stops was to see Tricia Sterling in her office on the Sterlings' mansion of a float house. Her father, Dave Sterling, was becoming one of the wealthiest men in Canada. He had worked his company up from very humble beginnings. His transparency and straightforward way of doing business were proving to be very popular. Some years ago, the Sterling Brothers Company had expanded into the United States, starting in Washington State. When I first arrived at Stuart Island, the rumour was that Dave's company was well on its way to having its first yearly billion-dollar gross.

He kept a summer place at Stuart Island for the use of his family, friends, and business associates. When they purchased the large property, it already had a house, boatsheds, and other buildings. Every summer, they also brought the big white float house up from Vancouver for their guests, while Dave and his family used the buildings on shore. The Sterlings quietly spent a great deal of money renovating and creating new amenities. The previous summer, they had installed a tennis court.

Tricia's small office on the float house was just by the front door. I approached their dock, tucked in behind their yacht and small runabout, and tied my boat off. Then I walked to the doorway and leaned in.

Tricia looked up from her desk. "Hey, Dave, welcome back! Another season getting started, eh? Making the usual rounds?"

She paused.

"Listen, why don't you go say hello to my dad? I don't want to get into a conversation and then have it interrupted. I'm waiting for a radio phone call from Vancouver that might come in any minute."

There was a kind of mischievous twinkle in her eyes that got my attention. "You should find Dad up on the tennis court. I'm sure he'll be happy to see you."

The ramps around the float house that allowed their guests to walk to shore hadn't been set up yet. I motored over to the tie-up dock along shore and tied off again. The walk up to the tennis court curved around the scenic shoreline. Being able to spend time here was one of the perks of guiding for the family. The Sterlings were very generous to the people working for them. The guides were certainly no exception; end-of-the-trip parties were a common ritual. There was a volleyball court, and at the end of last summer, a couple of the guides had a chance to try out the new tennis court. I wasn't much good at tennis, but I could lounge around wearing white outfits with the best of them.

As I stepped through the gate past the tall fence surrounding the court, I saw a lone figure, like a penitent, down on their hands and knees at the far side. I quickly realized it was Dave Sterling, facing away from me, bent over and absorbed in a task that required an intense focus with something miniscule. As I walked toward him, I watched him pick up a tiny object and put it in a bowl beside him, over and over again. Before I got too close, not wanting to surprise him, I cleared my throat loudly.

"Mr. Sterling, I didn't want to sneak up on you."

He continued with his task, so engrossed I wondered if he heard me.

"Tricia said you were up here. She thought I should say hello."

Still no response. As I approached the kneeling figure, I strained to see past his shoulder. A bucket sat not far from the bowl. Whatever he was picking up was so small that even as I got closer, I could not make it out.

When I arrived at his side, I could hear him muttering to himself, almost having a conversation, it seemed. I had to wait until the conversation offered a pause.

"What is it you are trying to do, exactly?"

He looked up.

"Oh, sorry, Dave! I just get lost. This damn thing. My mind just wanders away. I have been at it since this morning, and it feels like I have hardly made any headway at all."

I honestly didn't know what might constitute headway in whatever it was he was doing. He didn't seem to be accomplishing anything at all, though I couldn't really point that out.

"Mind if I ask—"

He cut me off before I got to the obvious question.

"Oh, it's really stupid. And my own damn fault."

He straightened up, sitting back on his heels. He waved his arms to indicate the offending problem.

"We put this tennis court in last year—you know that. What you might not know is that we can't keep a grass court growing properly up here. We had to install this surface; it's really state-of-the-art. It is designed to mimic a grass court and the way the ball responds on a grass court."

He rubbed his hand over the court surface much the same way you might stroke a favourite animal.

"It's a special Astroturf, a little longer than the regular. It looked like a big, green shag carpet when it was laid down. Then we barged in bags of this special sand that settles down into the Astroturf so that only the very ends of it are poking through. The people that have played on it so far really like it. I've quite enjoyed it myself."

Mr. Sterling realized he was stroking the court surface and pulled his hand away.

"It is like you have recreated Wimbledon right here on Stuart Island," I said, with no irony intended. It was kind of impressive the lengths Mr. Sterling had gone to create the tennis experience he was looking for. I didn't want to know how much it must have cost.

"Yes, Wimbledon. At least, I had that surface, until I almost ruined it completely."

"What happened?"

"Oh, I was in a hurry the last time I was up here. There is a cover for the court to stop this from happening, and I was just going too fast to set it up properly. That corner over there"—he pointed to the one he was working toward—"that corner wasn't lashed down properly and got blown up by the wind. The fir needles from the trees all around us blew over the uncovered part of the court. Lucky for me, it wasn't the whole thing, otherwise I would be here all summer doing this. It is only this one corner, but it has already taken me hours."

I took another look at the surface of the court. Once I knew what to look for, I realized the enormity of the task. The sand itself wasn't brown, it was a lovely golden yellow. It was the volume of fir needles that had settled on it that made it look brown.

"Oh, I see. Now I get it. Wow, so many fir needles! That's a huge amount of work. Can I, uh—can I help you?"

He shook his head slowly.

"No, Dave, I couldn't ask you to do this. I couldn't ask anybody to do this, even if I was going to pay them. It's all on me; I am the idiot responsible, so I am the idiot I hired to fix it."

"Couldn't you use a vacuum? I bet those new portable Dirt Devils they've just come out with—wouldn't they do the job?"

"Yeah, I've tried a couple of other ways. The vacuum sucks up the sand too. And a broom can't differentiate either. It also pushes the sand and the needles all together in a heap. Makes it worse."

I didn't know quite what to say. Before the silence got too awkward, he continued.

"So, Tricia must have sent you here."

"She said she was waiting for a phone call from Vancouver."

"You seem like a smart guy, Dave. You must have figured out by now there is no phone call coming from Vancouver. Tricia has inherited her mother's sense of humour all right. I am quite sure she is down there thoroughly enjoying herself."

"Seems like an odd sense of humour."

"It's payback. I guess you haven't heard the roller skate story yet. Don't worry, you'll hear the whole sad story soon enough." He sighed and looked toward the float house with fondness. His daughter was just like her mother.

"So, no doubt you are looking for some hours?" The change of subject was not lost on me. I was curious about the roller skates, but it seemed wise to be patient. I didn't actually learn the story until several seasons later.

"I was going to talk with Tricia when she got off the radio telephone."

"I'm bringing up some employee groups over the next couple of months. We would love to have you do some guiding for them, depending on your availability, of course. Let Tricia know I said so."

"Thank you, Mr. Sterling, I appreciate it. I'll see Tricia on the way out."

"And, Dave, you don't need to keep calling me Mr. Sterling," said Mr. Sterling. "Dave will do just fine, Dave."

"Okay, thanks, Mr. Sterling—uh, Dave."

As he bent back over his bowl, he looked up at me again.

"And, Dave? This little situation will just be between us, okay?"

"For sure! This—this will be our little secret."

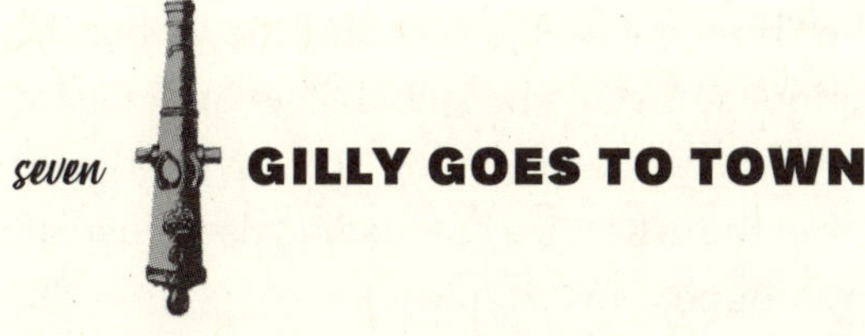

seven GILLY GOES TO TOWN

HERBERT WAS INSISTENT—NELSON had to help him load the frozen cougar onto his float plane for the return trip to Seattle. Never mind that for the last few days, Gilly had been hauling the poor thing in and out of the freezer, where it lay on top of most of the dinner menu. Gilly could probably have lugged the frozen carcass down the dock and onto the plane all by herself.

The result, with Nelson now being otherwise occupied, was that the first big shop of the season fell to Gilly to do. A long list of supplies had to be fetched from the biggest nearby town, Campbell River, over on Vancouver Island. Gilly sat down the night before and organized her extensive list according to the floor plan of the main supermarket.

When Nelson went on these trips to town, they always caused him a great deal of anxiety. Afterward, he would often disappear into the workshop and not talk to anyone for a couple of days. Gilly didn't see what the big deal was. When she lived on Read Island, she had made dozens of such trips. Construction supply trips while she was building her house, and grocery runs at least every couple of weeks. Shopping for the resort might mean a longer list and a better class of food selection, but otherwise it was hardly any different.

Gilly was up early the next morning. She kissed the still sleeping Nelson on the cheek before she left. She grabbed her packsack, loaded the night before with a few things she thought might prove useful. The lodge's freight boat was all gassed up and ready to go. She was going to enjoy running the big boat by herself as far as Heriot Bay on Quadra Island. The Coast Guard channel had news of a small craft warning, so Gilly was going to take the ferry from the other side of Quadra Island instead of going all the way around into Campbell River.

As she pulled away from the dock, it started to rain, the drops clattering against the outside of the cabin. Gilly liked watching them splash onto the freight boat's windshield. She had to admit, there were times when a windshield would have been a welcome addition to her own runabout, especially in the winter. This boat had a padded seat for the captain's chair and headphones for the cassette player, and even a heater! It was all quite luxurious.

The bad weather helped Gilly make good time to Heriot Bay. No pods of orcas or bears appeared on the beach; such distractions always slowed her progress. She docked at the government wharf. She changed out of her gumboots into some proper driving shoes, grabbed her bag with the shopping list, and headed to the truck parked along the road. Gilly made it to the other side of Quadra just as the ferry was pulling into the terminal.

The grocery store in Campbell River was busy. It was that time of year; Gilly wasn't the only one shopping for a resort or perhaps a tree planting camp. She worked her way down her list, aisle by aisle. She easily filled one cart and grabbed another, pushing one and trailing the other behind her. Even so, she couldn't see why this was so difficult that Nelson so frequently returned home traumatized.

When she got to the checkout, she realized she had forgotten something important.

People were already lined up behind her. She couldn't abandon the two full carts of groceries to go looking for her missing item; she'd ask someone to get it for her while her carts went through the till. To make things slightly more awkward, the till was being run by the store manager, a man. The checkouts were all so busy the manager must have opened another one to speed things up.

When it was Gilly's turn at the till, she cleared her throat and said in a quiet voice, "Hi. Um, I forgot to get one thing. I'm wondering if you could ask someone to get it for me."

The manager's job was to take care of his customers, and he took that job very seriously.

"What can I get for you, young lady?" he asked pleasantly.

The Young Lady spoke so quietly that the manager had to lean in to hear her.

"I need a couple of boxes of Tampax. Make it three—it's going to be some time before I get back to town."

The manager straightened up, all efficiency and speed.

"Not a problem," he said in a loud voice, the voice of a manager used to getting things done, "What size do you need?"

"Um, regular, regular would be fine." People behind her were watching, noticing the line's holdup. Gilly was beginning to turn a little red.

The manager grabbed the microphone for the store's PA system. "Moffat," he yelled into it. "I need you get me three boxes of Tampax for Till Four!"

Almost immediately, Moffat appeared. A lanky boy in an apron, he stood a head taller than those around him. By now, everyone's attention was on the little drama unfolding at Till Four.

The manager's voice over the PA system must have been a bit muffled. Moffat didn't have all the information he needed.

"What kind do you want?" he asked. His skinny frame housed a booming voice that reverberated through the now quiet store. "You want the kind you can push in with your thumb or the ones you need to bang in with a hammer?"

The manager looked puzzled for a moment, then a look of genuine horror spread across his affable face.

"Moffat, you idiot, not thumbtacks—Tampax!" He repeated it twice more for added emphasis, or perhaps just to make sure Moffat heard it correctly this time. "Tampax! Tampax! I'm talking feminine hygiene products, over there in Aisle Six, in the pharmacy section. Regular size."

Moffat turned around and quickly disappeared. Gilly wished she could disappear along with him. In fact, if a Stuart Island whirlpool had opened at her feet at that moment, she would have gladly let it swallow her whole.

When Gilly finally got back to the resort and the groceries were all properly put away, she disappeared into the cabins. A frenzy of cleaning and making beds followed.

It might not have been the first time someone had made that mistake—after all, the words did sound very much alike, especially over a garbled public address system in a busy grocery store. It probably won't be the last time that mistake is made either. However, this time it happened to Gilly. She didn't talk to anyone for a couple of days.

eight THE MUSSEL HUNTERS

I WAS AT the gas dock when the *Texas Tea* showed up, much earlier than expected. I was there picking up the propane for the cabin. The propane barge had been in and I swapped my two empties for a couple of refills. I stopped what I was doing and watched the arrival of the yacht with some interest.

The skipper seemed to know what he was doing. It was slack tide, and he nestled the yacht into the dock easily. There was no frenzy of shouted orders, no deckhands dodging about looking for tie-up lines and throwing worried glances at the water. The skipper did it all himself while the owner and a couple of his buddies watched from the deck.

As soon as the yacht hit the dock, the owner of *Texas Tea* wanted to go fishing. Troutbreath turned to me, and I knew my fresh propane tanks weren't going anywhere yet. Since Troutbreath wanted Lawrence to work this boat for the summer, he went to fetch him too. He found Lawrence on the back porch of the kitchen talking to Baba about grease.

Lawrence soon joined me, his boat already moored in his special spot near the gas dock. We quickly had three fishermen between our boats. They were painfully eager. We made a quick stop at the Reserve Box and then we were off.

A small flood tide was beginning to set up in the Second Hole. It wasn't too challenging for a rookie like Lawrence, so we dropped our lines. Hopefully we could start things off with a couple of salmon. It wasn't long before Lawrence and his two guests picked one up and followed it out into the tide.

Meanwhile, I was out with the *Texas Tea* owner, Brant, who was fishing by himself. He wanted to know about everything. Of course, his idea of everything was quite different than mine. I guess he was interested in how other people managed their businesses because he was a businessman. He was from Idaho, and I soon learned that his boat wasn't called *Texas Tea* because he had discovered oil. He ran the largest asphalt paving company in Idaho and eastern Washington State. He had numerous contracts to maintain and build the interstate roads. He was quick to point out that he came from humble origins, which, he said, might be why he identified so much with Jed Clampett—the reason for the name of his boat.

Unlike Jed Clampett, he sure liked to talk about business. There we were, floating around the Second Hole, a giant water-carousel ride, surrounded by forest, mountains, and tidal rapids. People were catching salmon, and the trees were filled with eagles, or at least the mechanical eagles we had installed, rather than any real ones, who could never be counted on to appear. Despite being surrounded by far more interesting subjects, I was answering Brant's questions about work. More specifically, I was explaining how I calculated year-over-year amortization of my class-eight deductions. Brant was fascinated.

"You should come work for me," he said. "You know more about that stuff than most of the people I've got working in my company!"

I had learned to ignore such suggestions. Brant was so interested in Canadian tax law, he didn't even notice when the tip of his rod started bouncing. By then, the Second Hole was getting a little crowded, and I was only too happy to steer the fish out into the tide after Lawrence. It was a nice little spring salmon, about twelve pounds or so, a "smiley." We played it down to Machine Shop Bay, where we could find some quieter water. The fish was tired by the time we got to the back eddy, where scooping it up into the net was no trouble.

Lawrence and his two guys pulled up beside us as I was putting the lid back onto the fish box.

"How big was your fish?" Brant yelled as they got close.

"About the same as the one you guys just pulled in."

Lawrence's voice carried across the water without him needing to shout.

"We have enough salmon for the barbecue tonight," Brant yelled again. "What do you two think?"

"Lawrence was telling us about all the mussels around here. How about we get a bucket of those," one of his buddies yelled back.

"What do you say, Dave? You know a place to get mussels around here?"

We weren't far from the entrance to Hole-in-the-Wall, whose shore was covered in them. It was a scenic run, and with the motor wide open, I wouldn't need to answer questions about Canadian tax laws.

It didn't take long to get there. The moment our boats glided up onto the gravel beach, one of the guys in Lawrence's boat stood up. He had a bucket and shovel in his hands, like a small child about to spend a day at the beach. Before Lawrence or I could say anything, he jumped out of the boat and started sprinting along the beach, right into the middle of the mussel bed. As he ran, orange pieces of mussel splashed up onto his bright yellow yachting boots. Lawrence and I both winced at the crunching sound. The man stopped, looked around him, and then turned back to face us.

"So, where's these mussels at?" he shouted.

Lawrence shook his head. I thought I heard the hint of a sigh.

"You know you're standing on 'em, eh?" Lawrence was calm and patient, as though he was talking to a small child. What he said and the way he said it pinned the man to the spot. "Just try walking back slowly. Set your feet into the footprints you made getting there. We don't want to squish any more of them."

The man proved capable of being told what to do. He picked his way carefully toward us and managed to make it back without doing more damage. Once we were all back together, I filled the bucket with seawater, and Lawrence patiently showed his two guys how to select the best mussels. It didn't take long for them gather a good helping for dinner that night. The man with the shovel seemed disappointed he didn't get to use it.

On the run back, I glanced occasionally at Brant, who sat quietly on the bench. Here was a man trying to reap the rewards of all his hard work. He had grown his business from patching people's driveways to being where he was today. He had lucrative contracts to maintain state highways and could afford to buy something he had always coveted: the luxury yacht we were heading for. He seemed happy and content with life. The struggles he had overcome only made life that much sweeter. He knew there were many people who wanted to be just like him.

I didn't want to be Brant, though. I knew what he was going to discover when our boat ride was over. While Brant was the proud owner of a brand-new Cape Flattery yacht, that purchase was a fateful one. He had opted for the fifty-five-footer, as opposed to the slightly more upscale sixty-foot model, a decision made after comparing prices and talking with his accountant. The large price difference hadn't seemed worth the extra five feet.

Sadly, I knew what that meant. Troutbreath had a pretty strict protocol when it came to the hierarchy of moorage. Only boats sixty feet or better were given the preferred tie-ups on the main dock. From the main dock, a spacious ramp led directly to the dining room and lounge. People could proceed at their leisure and make a carefully considered impression.

The smaller yachts and sailboats were banished to the unfashionable boathouse docks. They were older and moved more, especially with the pull of the tide. If you weren't used to things moving under foot, walking proved to be a daunting task. You ended up staggering about like—well, like a drunken sailor. As you stumbled along, quite often you did so under the knowing gaze of the resort guides, who used the same route to get to their dining room or the guide shack. From the docks, a narrow ramp led up to the front deck of the boathouse. An arrow below the word RESTAURANT pointed to a path that emptied out onto the side of the kitchen. As you walked past, you also fell under the knowing gaze of kitchen staff enjoying a cigarette.

To add insult to injury, you also had to pass by one of Mr. Carrington's favourite pieces of art.

When he had begun overhauling his prized Fisheries vessel, one of the first things he removed was the toilet seat in the head. A previous owner had cast the seat and its lid in fibreglass resin. They had carefully arranged a display of tropical seashells, a couple of exotic starfish, and even a seahorse, forever preserved inside the clear, although unfortunately urine-coloured, polymer, which had hardened into something quite impressive but also very heavy—the main reason it was removed.

However, Mr. Carrington was so taken by it that he tacked it up on the outside wall of the boathouse next to the helpful arrow sign. It was hung upside down, so that the seat gaped open like a mouth with a tongue sticking out. People could often be seen scurrying past it, trying to avert their eyes. Sometimes screams seemed to emanate out of this mouth. Perhaps it was only the shrill shriek, channeling through the seat and out along the lid, of someone's high-speed saw cutting their ironwood gunnels to length, wood as hard as steel. Other times, it seemed to offer the gruff sounds of a belt sander. Or sometimes, the poor owners of the under-sixty-footers would be subject, like the Eloi encountering the mysterious workings of the Morlocks, to the thumping rumble of hidden machinery from deep inside the boatshed. These sounds were all somehow focused by the wall art, with a mysterious purpose unknown to the casual visitor.

No matter how much someone might whine and moan about their location or how much money they might try to offer, Troutbreath had insulated himself well. There was no argument to be made. It was a simple matter of overall length. Size really did matter. I knew Brant would put a brave face on it. Eventually, though, between the small size of his cherished yacht and having to mingle with people on sailboats, he too would be carrying his eyes downcast. He would have that same slow shuffle instead of the walk of pride, worn down like the rest of the motorboat owners on this dock of shame.

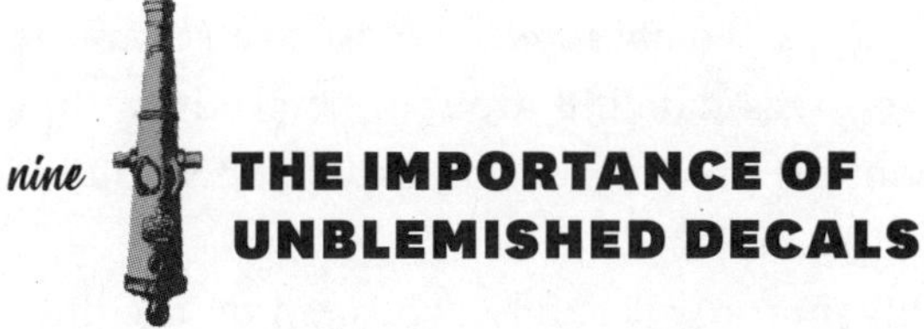

nine THE IMPORTANCE OF UNBLEMISHED DECALS

THE WIVES OF the men from the *Texas Tea* were waiting for us when we got back to the dock. They had flown in from Seattle while we were out collecting mussels. I could already hear some grumbling about where the yacht was "parked." I listened quietly as Brant promised to speak to the skipper about a more convenient location. However, I was pretty sure Troutbreath and the skipper had already come to an understanding.

The plan was for everyone to go out first thing next morning. However, Brant took me aside, a slightly pleading look in his eyes. He wanted to go out for an evening tide. While his buddies were happy to enjoy some evening beverages on the boat, he wanted to take his wife fishing. He was hoping, I suppose, that a quiet boat ride and a glorious sunset might lighten the mood.

When I got back to our dock, I found Vop in something of a panic.

Vop had arrived on the freight boat earlier that afternoon. He was expected to be another of the guides for the *Texas Tea*, so his arrival was timely, if a bit late. The skipper of the freight boat had to use the cargo crane to load Vop's new motor carefully onto the end of our dock.

It was a brand-new fifty-horsepower Mercury outboard motor, 160 pounds of fresh paint, unblemished decals, and delicate tiller arms and gear shifts. Vop had upgraded to stainless for the prop, which added a few extra pounds.

The skipper was extremely careful not to do any damage. The fact that Vop was dancing around, helpfully yelling instructions about his precious decals, had no effect on the skipper's approach to his job.

As soon as his motor was safely deposited on the dock, Vop had thrown himself into getting ready for the next morning's tide. He had worked up quite a sweat. It was such a spectacle that the skipper of the freight boat had found the time to dawdle and observe.

Vop's boat had been stored upside down, under the cover of the boatshed, beside our cabin. So far, he had managed to flip his boat over and then manhandle it down to the shoreline. It was painfully obvious that getting it to move over the rocky beach was more difficult than he expected, and the tide was out a little farther than he would have liked. Vop cursed the people who published tide tables.

He persisted, though; he had no other choice. At one point, he stopped, walked back to the boathouse, and returned carrying what appeared to be a sheet of plywood. Vop looked quite pleased with himself, acting like a man who, with a little ingenuity, had found a solution. The freight boat skipper had observed that it was now much easier for Vop to manhandle the boat down to the water. In no time, Vop's boat was floating at the end of the dock, conveniently tied up beside the new motor. The skipper reluctantly said his goodbyes and set off for his next destination.

I FOUND VOP lying on his back on the floor of his boat, his head under the seat mount. Apparently, what he was doing there made him loudly reconsider his career choices. He had two new guest chairs to install. The guest chairs on our guide boats took some serious punishment from the many larger-bodied guests who used them. Replacing them was a notoriously frustrating job.

There was a time when a guide could get by with a couple of rounds of firewood and a lifejacket on top for seating, but that had all changed. The clients were starting to get more demanding. This change could not be blamed on Gilly and Heidi and the thought and care they put into their boats. Rather, the two women anticipated such demands and showed us the right way to respond.

As expected, Vop was having a hard time. His new seats, unlike the two broken fibreglass bucket seats they were replacing, were high-density foam cushions inside leather-like vinyl. They even had arms containing the same foam. He was taking things to a new level.

All he had to do was get the holes lined up.

The bottoms of the chairs had to be fitted with swivels. The guests might need to, well, swivel. There was a complex system of bolts and their corresponding holes. The swivel had a top and a bottom plate. The top plate was lag-bolted into the bottom of the chair, and the bottom plate had a hole in each corner for the bolts that held the chair to the boat. It was important to hang the bolts from the bottom plate first, before you secured the swivel to the chair. The two plates were so close together you couldn't put the bolts into the bottom one with the swivel already on the chair. Vop had found that out the hard way, having had to remove the swivel from the chair once already. On Vop's boat were two open-sided fibreglass boxes with four, hopefully matching, boltholes drilled into them, where the chairs on their swivels were supposed to go. The trick was to get the bolts hanging down from the swivel to line up with those holes, all the while balancing a rather heavy deluxe chair to keep all the bolts hanging straight at the same time. It was a job that could reduce a grown man to tears.

I was on a tight schedule, but it was fascinating to watch Vop prostrate himself for the sake of bigger tips. Vop was only too happy to take a short break to join me on the dock.

We both looked down at his new motor. It still lay there, 160-plus pounds of truculent metal. Vop had spent a great deal of time thinking about what to do next, and he went into a long explanation. It involved balance, leverage, making sure we always had secure footing—here Vop stopped in mid-sentence to change the subject. I had only just noticed the word "we."

"What have you got on your feet?"

I had my black, formal clamdiggers on due to the afternoon's activity of gathering mussels.

"Those things should be okay," Vop announced. I realized his plans involved my help.

He saw the pained look I was giving him. "Come on, don't look at me like that. You're always wearing those flimsy canvas things, like you're a dancer in some kind of pirate musical!"

I knew how much his decals meant to him, but while I was willing to stand there for inspection, Vop needed to expect some eye rolling.

We lifted the motor upright. While I stood on the dock holding up the motor, Vop got onto his boat. Together, we inched the motor to the edge of the dock and lifted it up onto the tie-up rail.

We caught our breath, then lowered the motor slowly until it stood on the floor of his boat. Once the boat had stopped rocking and I could let go of the motor, Vop held it upright while I joined him on board. Between us, we walked it back to the spot where it would sit on the transom.

The next part was a little tricky. We had to tip the motor toward the bow and lift it out over the water to settle its bracket over the top of the transom.

The boat heaved and rocked, and we had to steady ourselves. We were both holding a great deal of weight. The motor could slip out of our grip and scrape down the back of the boat or even pitch out of it entirely. The motor caught the top of the bracket. We had to jostle it, then lift it up and over one more time. We couldn't even see where it needed to go. Fortunately, we felt it catch and then drop into place.

Vop quickly tightened down the clamps on the bracket as hard as he could by hand. A couple of bolts still had to be fastened to secure the motor to the transom, but that could all be done later. For now, it was enough that the motor was in place—and all the paint and decals were still pristine.

I had to leave Vop to finish getting his boat ready. I still had to head out for the evening.

BY THE TIME I got back to the cabin much later that night, Vop had passed out from exhaustion.

The next morning, over coffee, I told Vop that Brant, the owner of the *Texas Tea*, wanted Vop to take him and his wife, Gloria, out soon. "He wanted me to pass on the message. So, you know, no pressure."

"Good thing I finally got my seats in then." Vop sounded fairly pleased with himself.

His self-congratulatory manner continued most of the morning. On a hunch, he took his two clients north from Big Bay and stopped at the Log Dump for the start of the flood tide there. It paid off with a couple of eighteen-pound spring salmon. The conversation flowed easily, and Brant and Gloria quickly transitioned from calling him "Ivor" to using his nickname, Vop.

Gloria asked, "Your nickname is Vop? That's kind of unusual. How did you come by it?"

"My last name is Vopnstrom, and it turned out the postal code here starts with VOP. Everyone just started calling me V-o-p."

"So you don't pronounce the zero."

"Well, Vop is close enough."

At this point, Vop didn't care what she called him; things were going so well.

"We've got a couple of nice fish in the boat, Ivor." Brant wasn't about to try his luck at pronouncing Vop's nickname just yet. "Maybe it's time to head back for lunch. Would you care to join us? It will be kind of a potluck."

Vop could think of nothing better to cap off such a great first session. He invited the two of them to turn their comfortable new chairs to face forward. Unlike his old, fixed seats, the new ones could now swivel around completely. Vop had invested heavily. He wanted his guests to have the luxury of seeing where they were going, rather than where they had just been.

He smiled broadly as he pulled out of the Log Dump's back eddy and turned toward Big Bay. The flood was running full by now, but it wasn't a big tide. It was by far much quicker to run the Arran Rapids back to Big Bay than to go all the way around Stuart Island. Vop didn't want to put Brant and Gloria through such a long and tedious ride, and besides, he was excited about lunch.

Still smiling, with Brant and Gloria looking very comfortable, Vop took the usual approach along the Stuart Island side of the rapids. The tide flow into Bute Inlet is constricted by the narrow opening between the mainland and the island. As it rushes in, it drops like water through a chute. It runs fast and smooth to start, but as the gap narrows, the smooth flow meets the existing water in the back eddies and it all starts churning into a mess of white water, random upwellings, and deep, vicious whirlpools. The idea is to work your way along the shore of the island, through the back eddies, where you can avoid the most dangerous water.

A guide has to watch for one particular spot, marked by rocks jutting into the streaming water, where the incoming tide collides sharply with the water already in the channel. This meeting creates a pressure ridge, the height of which depends on the size of the tide. Conditions at that one spot are predictable, making it the safest place to cut from the back eddy into the main channel. However, even on a relatively small tide like this one, it can be hard to see what is lurking on the other side of the ridge.

As you pick your way around all the turbulence, you must watch for that meeting and the opportunity to make the cut. You pull back on your speed enough to hold position in the back eddy. You stay alert and watchful, waiting for the right time. There might be a bad unexpected whirlpool or a piece of drifting wood floating in the current. Sometimes, you just rely on your instincts, gun the engine, and go for it.

Now, while Vop might have been smiling as he approached the chute of the rapids, he did not take any of it for granted. These were some of the most dangerous tidal rapids in the world. If you got pulled into that whirlpool, or if you collided with that piece of driftwood that stopped you dead, you would be left vulnerable. Even driving into a tide-generated air bubble on the surface would make your propeller spin uselessly. Anything that stopped your forward progress and made you lose control—well, it would be hard to recover from that. Falling into the grip of the rapids took only a moment.

Vop always pushed those possibilities into the back of his mind. After all, he had done this dozens of times, and he was quite comfortable in these kinds of conditions.

He carefully picked his spot to cross over the ridge and gunned the motor. This part always gave him a rush of excitement. He turned the engine sharply, so the boat would turn into the flow, ready to sit in the strong current coming at them on the other side. He felt his boat dig into the water. His bow pitched up, the water acting like a ramp. Vop felt momentarily, exhilaratingly weightless as the boat dropped onto the other side of the ridge. As the boat splashed down, the water flowing through the main channel immediately tried to push him back the way he came.

Vop gave the engine just a little more gas for some control and the boat surged forward. He was now riding the surging current, going uphill in a very real sense. The water flowed past his boat at perhaps eight or ten knots and had dropped about five or six feet from the entrance. Vop, seeing no debris coming toward him, confidently opened the throttle wide.

As he began to power up the hill of water, something under his hand felt like it had come loose.

Vop had never experienced anything like this before. His left arm, holding the tiller handle of his brand new, shiny, outboard motor, began to rise into the air. It took him a moment to understand exactly what was causing this to happen. He looked back to see that the engine was now floating above and a little behind the transom. The boat was no longer attached to the engine, except for the gas line and electrical cables.

A cold chill settled over Vop. He knew what he had forgotten to do.

In the haste to get his boat into the water and ready for guests, he had forgotten to install the two heavy-duty stainless-steel bolts through the transom—the bolts that locked his engine into place. The clamps he had tightened by hand were by themselves not enough to fight the power of the water. Now the only thing keeping the boat and motor together, aside from the fragile gas line and battery cables, was Vop's grip on the tiller arm.

Vop's smile was now frozen in place. His two very important guests kept looking back at him, to share the exhilaration of being in such fast water. If Vop showed even the slightest concern about anything in a spot like this, his guests might panic, especially when Vop was himself close to panic.

He did his best to convince himself that outboard engines often floated in the air on their own accord. The possibility that his new engine could simply drop off the stern of his boat was too dreadful to consider. The smile was going to remain in place no matter what.

He casually reached back with his right hand. It put him in a weird, contorted position, but he kept smiling. There was a hand-hold built into the back of the engine cover. His hand folded around it and held on, clinging to the engine cowl with a ferocity that surprised even him. He was happy to discover he could now direct the errant engine back to touch the transom. All he had to do was lift the motor a few inches to clear the clamp bracket and settle it back down. There was nothing else for it.

With a desperate heave, he lifted the engine up. The clamp got stuck. His heart in his mouth, Vop had to let the engine drift back to free it. This meant giving over some control of the engine to the rushing water. Before the water could carry it too far, Vop heaved up again. He moved the engine forward slightly, so the clamp was positioned over the transom. Then Vop put his full weight onto it pushing down. Over the sounds of the running motor and roar of the rapids, he felt more than heard the reassuring clunk as the motor fell back into place.

The motor was still not secure. Vop was the only thing keeping it in place. He lay sprawled over the top of the engine, using the full weight of his body against the force of the water. He balanced and held on as best as he could, then carefully turned the throttle and powered up as much as he dared.

He was beginning to put some distance between his boat and the dangerous water behind him. That realization gave him some relief. All he had to do was hang on to the engine and not fall into the water.

All this squirming around wasn't going unnoticed. Vop's guests were now fully turned in the new chairs, looking back at him. He knew he had to say something. He did have one advantage. This was their first time going through the Arran Rapids. They would have no idea, really, if this was normal or not. Vop smiled down at them from his position on top of the motor, like some kind of lunatic Cheshire cat.

Then he started pointing out points of scenic interest.

"As you can see here, we are actually going uphill." He had to yell to be heard. "That's how fast the water is rushing past us into the inlet back there."

He had to point with his chin rather than let go of the motor.

Vop managed to ride the engine past the entrance to the Arrans and found a quiet back eddy. On the pretext of switching his gas tanks, he discreetly tightened down the clamps once more. He took a longer route home, keeping to the gentlest back eddies. On edge the entire way, Vop was relieved to finally pull into the dock beside the *Texas Tea* and drop off his customers. He found a way to excuse himself from lunch and headed home.

I GOT BACK for lunch shortly after Vop. I found him in the back of his boat, again wrestling with his new engine.

"Hey, Vop. Umm... what are you doing?"

I stood looking down at him from the dock. He was flushed from the exertion.

"Are you okay?"

"No, not really. I might eventually be okay, but not anytime soon," he replied enigmatically.

"See these?" he continued, holding up two long stainless-steel bolts. "I got so busy installing those damn seats"—he gestured toward them in a very derogatory manner—"that I, uh... neglected to install the bolts that kept the motor on the boat."

His voiced dropped to a whisper.

"And it lifted up off the transom while I was running the Arrans... with Brant and Gloria!"

"It did what?" I was a little stunned. "What do you mean by 'lifted off,' exactly?"

"I mean 'lifted off,' as in the engine came right up and completely off the boat. The only thing holding onto it was the gas line, battery cables, and my hand on the tiller."

I shook my head.

"Seriously, man," said Vop, a little plaintively.

"What the hell! What did you do?"

"That's the thing—what else *could* I do? I had just jumped the rip into the main channel. There was nothing but white water and whirlpools behind us. My left hand was the only thing keeping the motor from falling off completely. I had to keep the boat going to get away from the rapids, so I reached back with my right arm and hoisted it. I lifted it back on! Then I laid on top of it. I rode it; I rode the motor until we were safe."

He looked at his former mount in disbelief.

"The part that freaks me out the most, though, is that I've been sitting here at the dock trying to do it again. My left hand on the tiller, my right arm reaching across." Vop demonstrated what that looked like. "As hard as I try, I can't even move it. I can't budge the damn motor. Here, you try it."

He stood up and gestured for me to take his place.

"No, I'll take your word for it. Remember, I helped you put it on last night. Wow! You must have been pumped full of adrenalin, man. I can't even imagine."

"It's okay, though. I don't think they noticed anything. I managed to stay pretty relaxed the whole time."

"I see you didn't damage any of the decals either." I tried to switch to a topic less fraught with adrenalin. "Is that a jar of Turtle Wax?" I said, pointing to a small jar of blueish-green paste on the floor of his boat.

Vop gave me a suspicious look. With his foot he nudged the Turtle Wax under a cloth.

"One of my boat customers distributes car cleaning products. He brought me up a case of it. Just came by a little while ago and dropped it off. It was more of a favour for Gilly, really."

"What are you guys going to do with a whole case of Turtle Wax?" It was an honest question.

"Uh... polish stuff," was the only answer Vop would give me. Then it was his turn to change the subject.

I knew there was more to the story than that, especially with Gilly involved. It was another one of Gilly's secrets she chose to share with Vop, no doubt because of his connections. He was my roommate, though. I would find out eventually. I could be patient, like water dripping onto a stone.

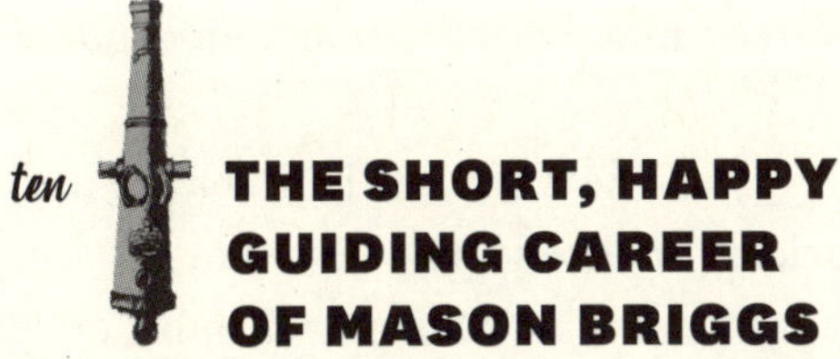

ten THE SHORT, HAPPY GUIDING CAREER OF MASON BRIGGS

UNFORTUNATELY FOR VOP, his guests did notice his troubles in the Arrans. At least Gloria did; she was from Seattle and had grown up on the water. She wasn't an expert, but she did know that outboard engines work better attached to the boat. She took Troutbreath aside and had a quiet chat with him. As much as she enjoyed fishing with Vop, she wouldn't be comfortable sending her friends and business partners out in his boat. Troutbreath could only agree with her. He was thankful she wanted to keep it quiet; even her husband didn't know that anything had happened.

Troutbreath would have preferred to hear the news from Vop rather than one of his guests. But worse than that, he needed to find another guide to work for the *Texas Tea*. Vop was lucky guides were so hard to come by, though, and the demand for them was growing. He saw a chance to make amends.

"I know a guy down on Cortes who has been bugging me to get him in with one of the resorts. He has his own boat and all the gear. He has been up here fishing for himself enough to know the water. I can put you in touch with him. His name is Mason Briggs."

OVER THE NEXT couple of weeks, I got to know Mason, maybe a little too well.

"You don't mind if Mason stays with us, do you, Dave?" Vop phrased it less as a question and more as a statement of fact. To be fair, there weren't many places for an independent guide to live.

Mason showed up early the next day. He had a brand-new, seventeen-foot Nantucket and all the best gear. I'm still not sure how he managed to afford it all. Mason was in his early twenties, like most of the guides. He wore a black leather vest over a bare chest and tight designer jeans. I recognized the label; it was one of the companies owned by my old fishing buddy Morris Goldfarb.

Mason liked to flick things. He wore his hair long, and he was always flicking it behind his ear. He smoked those little rum-dipped, wine-flavoured Colts with the white plastic tips, although he didn't smoke them as much as he flicked them. He would stand with his arms folded in front of him and then suddenly pull the thing out of his mouth and flick the ash off. He did this to make a point when he was talking, something he did quite often. When it burned low enough, Mason would flick the butt into the water, plastic tip and all.

Troutbreath and Vop went out fishing in the rapids with Mason. They caught a couple of nice springs, and by all reports Mason was competent enough with his boat-handling skills. Troutbreath was comfortable sending him out with people.

As it turned out, those skills wouldn't matter as much as you would expect. New guests arrived on the *Texas Tea* that afternoon. Troutbreath sent Lawrence, Mason, and a couple other guides to meet them on the dock. It was another party of Brant's relatives. Among them was his youngest sister. She seemed a little shy, as she appeared on the dock by herself.

It was almost as if she had been in hiding and was just now allowing herself to be seen in public.

"Are you all guides here?" she asked. "I'm Anna, Brant's little sister. I'm not much of a fisherperson. I would be kind of a challenge for one of you. Fortunately, it's just me."

Mason was up for the challenge and immediately stepped forward. He carefully flicked the ash off the end of his cigarillo and announced, "I'm a very patient guy. Why don't you come with me?"

She looked relieved that she didn't need to make the decision herself. Lately, her life had been nothing but one major decision after another. Divorce can be like that.

"That sounds about right. Is that your boat there beside you?"

We didn't see much of Mason after that.

THE TIDES WERE getting bigger as the moon advanced. We had to contend with crowded back eddies and tangled lines. All the while, the sun beat down mercilessly. The tides were building each day. Soon we were going to have some of the biggest tides of the year. Everything became more difficult, and even catching herring at night, when the stronger evening tides played havoc with the nets, was a challenge. The fishing holes were chaos as well. The rushing water caused more tangles, and a sudden surge might cause your line to snag on the rocks below.

While Vop and I were up and out for an early start, away from the crowds, or to jig for a couple dozen herring, Mason would still be sleeping. He would putter over to the *Texas Tea* for a leisurely brunch with Anna, and then they'd head out on the water. We would see the two of them as they ran past the fishing holes toward the beaches farther up Bute Inlet.

Brant's sister let her hair down and it flowed out behind her in blonde waves; Mason, at the tiller, had one of his Colts clamped firmly in his teeth.

One morning, as we waited for Brant's guests to get organized, Lawrence and I watched Mason slowly leave our dock at the cabin and start motoring over to the pub. Lately, this was Anna and Mason's preferred place for a quiet morning meal, just the two of them, their heads close together in conversation. There was more privacy at the pub, with all the busyness happening on Brant's yacht most days.

"I don't think those two are doing much fishing." Lawrence had also been observing their blossoming relationship.

"Yeah." I couldn't help but agree. "I haven't seen them in the rapids at all. There have been some sightings elsewhere, though. There are some nice white sand beaches just up the Bute. Great places for a picnic. You should ask Vop about those beaches. I am sure they hold a special place in his heart, what with falling trees and all."

"Probably all for the best." Lawrence shook his head knowingly. "They're not spending any time in the rapids. The water out there is getting intense, eh? Must have been one hell of a shock, Vop's engine lifting off in the Arrans like that. I would have loved to see the look on his face when it happened."

"Our friend Vop gets himself in some situations, all right." It was my turn to shake my head. "He's got a different facial expression for every one of them. He should never play poker."

"Still, these big tides don't seem to bother him much after all that happened."

"You'll find Vop doesn't spend much time in self-reflection." I turned to him. "You seem to be comfortable out there yourself—I mean, as a first-year guide."

"Well, you know, Big Jake takes all the new guys out. He showed me how to get in and out of the back eddies. We spent most of the time learning how to keep the boat over top of the lines, you know, to keep the lines at the right angle falling forward so you get the proper action on the herring. I'm even catching a few fish.

"Of course, I have spent all my life on the water in some sort of boat or another. I mean, look at me, I've got long arms, and kind of short legs, a low centre of gravity." Lawrence patted his stomach affectionately. "It's really what you want for being in small boats. It's almost like I was designed for it. Some guys are just too top heavy; they keep pitching forward out of the boat."

The idea made Lawrence break out in his usual wide grin and he started chuckling to himself. Our conversation was interrupted by the guests. Four of them appeared on the stern of the *Texas Tea* and started navigating the dangerous apparatus that was the gangplank down to the dock. It was time for me and Lawrence to head back out.

As the tides grew bigger, the fishing holes were turning into a seething tangled mess. It was almost impossible not to get crossed up. Everywhere you looked, boats were bumping together as the guides unwrapped tangled lines or returned lead weights. Sometimes it was easier just to cut off all the tangled lines and start again rather than spending too much time with those lines out of the water.

Everyone was getting frustrated. Constantly reeling up and letting line back down left your guests frustrated. Constantly having to cut more bait with one hand while steering the boat with the other left the guides frustrated. They ended up spattered in herring guts, herring scales, and herring slime, which the hot sun then cooked onto them. The haze of blue smoke given off by the overworked trolling motors hung in the air, making it difficult to breathe, and then…

And then, something, a feeling of a presence perhaps, made us all look up from our misery. There he was, Mason Briggs, a Colt cigarillo clamped securely in his teeth as he cruised past us, the choking wretches in the fishing hole staring after him. He sat comfortably in the deluxe stern seat of his Nantucket. The throttle of his brand-new, shining engine was opened wide, unblemished decals glistening in the same sun under which the rest of us sweltered.

Mason and his special guest glided effortlessly past the clogged fishing holes. They were headed up the main channel, past the back eddies and whirlpools. Brant's sister had her chair turned toward the bow, her hair unfurled and streaming in the wind. She was a vision, a figurehead from an old sailing ship come to life. We all sat in our boats, mouths agape, like peasants watching a procession of our betters.

Of course, sharing accommodations with Mason, you got to hear his side of things. According to Mason, he might not be dealing with dogfish or tangled lines, but he did have his own set of special problems.

"Oh man," he said, on one of the rare occasions when he was back at the cabin. "My gonch feels like sandpaper! My damn ass is so sunburned."

Mason flicked an ash off his cigarillo.

I looked up from tying leaders; the dogfish had been especially bad that day. Mason wore a ridiculous grin.

"Seriously? You really expect to play that for sympathy?"

Mason just looked away, shrugged his shoulders, and flicked some more ash.

A couple of days later, it was time for us to hand in our hours. We all squeezed into the galley of the *Texas Tea*: Mason, me, Lawrence, and a couple of the Big Bay guides who had filled in from time to time. The skipper and Brant were there, looking serious, as men do before they disperse a large amount of money. The two random Big Bay guides, who were paid out by way of Troutbreath, received a large tip in American twenties. They left with smiles on their faces. Lawrence's hours were handled the same way, but he had some idea of what was going to happen and stayed in the galley.

As independent guides, the boats paid us directly, along with a finder's fee to Troutbreath. He had to get something for putting up with us. My bill for Brant was straightforward. He paid it out in crisp American hundreds, carefully counted, and then he laid out another one for a tip.

Then we all turned to Mason.

With a shrug he pulled out a torn and crumpled piece of paper with some numbers on it and the date. Brant looked it over carefully.

"Mason," Brant said, after some consideration, "I knew you were a man with a certain skill set the first time I laid eyes on you. However, I didn't understand I was dealing with a true master of his craft, at least judging by how expensive you are. To put it bluntly, you must be the most expensive whore on the block! Don't get me wrong, I've had no complaints from my sister." I thought I saw Mason redden slightly. "But since my sister won't be back for the rest of the summer, your, uh, services will no longer be needed."

Brant paused to let it sink in. We witnessed the moment when Mason suddenly realized he might have lost his opportunity to work Stuart Island as a guide.

But Brant wasn't an unkind man. He continued, "You know, son, if you had even caught just a couple of fish, we could have looked the other way and kept you on."

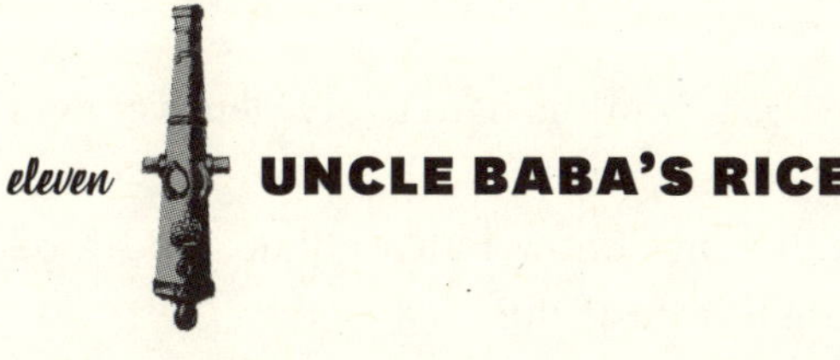

eleven UNCLE BABA'S RICE

A SHORT TIME LATER, Lawrence and I stood on the gas dock, watching Mason pull away. Word was already spreading. Mason's career had begun like a spectacular firework and exploded in the same manner. Enjoying the company of a guest wasn't the problem, so much. I had a look at his invoice. He had the guiding clock running even while he sat with Anna over a long brunch on the pub's balcony. It really wasn't done. It made him basically unemployable.

As he pulled away, we knew we were watching the birth of a legend. He motored far enough out from the gas dock so that he could open the throttle. His boat leapt up out of the water and he was gone.

"I would have given him a fish," said Lawrence into the silence that followed.

I knew Lawrence was as good as his word.

"That would have been very generous of you," I said.

"Oh, I don't know. You shouldn't be too surprised. My people"—and here Lawrence emphasized "my people" with a wink of his eye—"have a history of helping out with a fish or two when needed. It wouldn't be the first time."

I had a feeling there was a story to be told. Lawrence always seemed to talk about the past as though it was yesterday or just last week.

"Anyway, I hear Baba has some crème brûlées. I love that stuff!"

"It amazes me he has to work so hard to give leftover ones away." I could already taste them.

"These young kids don't know much about good food. Kind of sad, really. Shall we head up?"

"I'll join you in a bit. I've just got to tidy my boat up."

I'd noticed Old Man Lynwood farther down the dock. He was standing next to my boat, talking loudly with a couple of people.

As much fun as I was having with the *Texas Tea*, I did have other clients, and the Community Salmon Derby was only a couple of days away. Old Man Lynwood had been coming up to the island for years. I knew about him by reputation, but we had never even been introduced. As a long-standing member of the Seattle Yacht Club, he was one of the people who had popularized Stuart Island as the place to go. He was also one of the people who had helped develop the art of mooching in the rapids. His name was mentioned in debates about the origins of the cut-plug.

He often fished by himself and could be seen in a little green skiff. It was one of the very early motorized boats used up here. Its stern was designed with a place for a small motor. There were no seats, and Old Man Lynwood perched on a round of firewood with a life preserver on top of it. He had one rod holder on the starboard side. He would go drifting past the crowded holes on a mission all to himself. He watched the tip of his rod intently and played out line or reeled it in; he had memorized all the rocks and ridges below. He treated every dip and twitch of the rod tip as if it might be a monster salmon nibbling on his carefully prepared cut-plug.

I had heard that his family used to own the same cabin that Vop and I were in. Although he had a yacht now, a crew of people to run things, and enough money to do anything he wanted, all he wanted to do was fish. He had sold off the family business and now spent most of his time fishing. He would fly up to Alaska or northern BC, always looking for a world-record salmon. The entry into the Guinness Book of Records still eluded him.

No matter what else might be going on, he was always at Stuart Island for the derby. He had come close to winning it on several occasions, but that little engraved plaque, glued to a piece of bark, proved to be as elusive as a world-record tyee. That only seemed to make him pursue the title with greater fervour.

I got to my boat and stepped into it, casually sorting out the landing net. I knew Old Man Lynwood knew my name, but I was quite sure he couldn't pick me out from the rest of the guides. As I tidied, I listened in. He was talking with two skippers from the other yachts. Rather than gather any tips on his fishing preferences, I found myself listening in on a conversation about medical procedures for sun-damaged skin. Whatever the other two had done, Old Man Lynwood had to outdo them. His nose, the tops of his ears, and his forehead all had been whittled down to some extent, different types of skin damage removed in different ways.

They were just wrapping things up and returning to their respective yachts when Old Man Lynwood asked a final question.

"Say, have either of you guys seen Jacobs around? I thought he would be up here for the derby and all."

The two men both shook their heads as though there had been a death in the family.

"I guess you haven't heard," one of them said. "They think he was using his job at Boeing to steal secrets and sell them to the Russians. They found letters written in that squiggly Russian writing thanking him for what he had done. He tried to deny it at first, of course, but I always thought there was some truth to it."

"No, I hadn't heard that." Old Man Lynwood sounded shocked at the realization. "I know Boeing does military contract work. That could be very serious. Are they sure about it?"

"Yeah, they got him pretty much dead to rights—all of them letters. He must have been doing it for years. He finally opened up and admitted that was what he was doing," the other one added helpfully.

"Well, you know what they say." Old Man Lynwood summed it up succinctly. "It couldn't happen to a nicer fella!"

They all laughed and headed on their separate ways.

WHEN I FINALLY ARRIVED at the kitchen back porch, I noticed a couple of the shore staff waitresses leaving. They had the look of two people that had just won some kind of victory. Lawrence and Baba were sitting together on the porch watching them go and eating crème brûlée. They seemed highly amused. Baba shook his head.

"Ai-yi-yi... Campbell River girls, always drinking, smoking."

Baba was making gestures that mimicked the way they drank and smoked at the same time.

"Now they have big complaint about my cooking!"

This was a little hard to believe. Baba served the guides and shore staff the same thing he served the guests. It might be leftovers, but they were Baba's leftovers—the leftovers of a Blue Ribbon, Belgium-trained chef. He was the one who usually complained about the staff. In Belgium, being waitstaff was a respected career. They were an integral part of a fine dining experience. However, this was not Belgium.

"What could they possibly find wrong with your cooking?" I asked.

"They don't like my rice."

"You mean the saffron rice you always make, with the expensive saffron?"

"And not just any expensive saffron," Baba elaborated. "Only the best Spanish saffron is good for Baba's kitchen. Thirty dollars a gram!"

He rolled the "r" in the word gram.

"That's not good enough for them?" I was kind of incredulous.

"Ai-yi..." said Baba.

"I don't think they slow down long enough to taste anything." Lawrence sensed Baba's exasperation.

"It isn't the taste they complained about, though," Baba tried to explain. "It's the colour!"

"What?"

"Rice isn't supposed to be yellow." Baba put the complaint into the simplest terms possible. "They stormed in here and demanded 'normal' rice! They even brought in an example of what normal rice is supposed to look like."

Baba held up a box that said it contained converted white rice.

"'Ready in five minutes,'" he read, his nose wrinkling in distaste. "Baba now makes two kinds of rice. Those girls work hard, they try to learn. Okay, if they want white rice, I make them white rice. I just want to know, who is this Uncle Ben?"

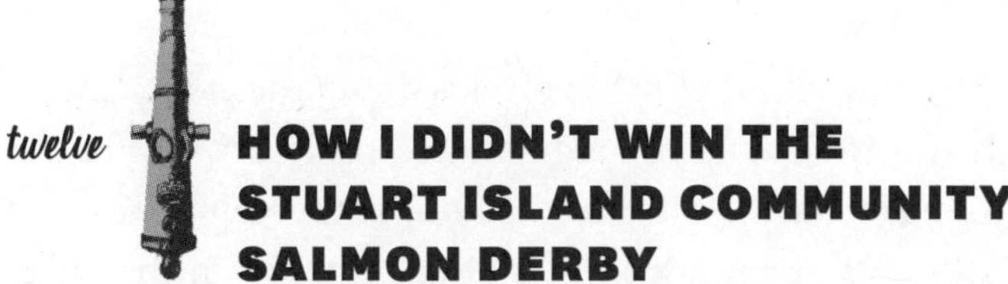

twelve HOW I DIDN'T WIN THE STUART ISLAND COMMUNITY SALMON DERBY

IT WAS THE NIGHT before the derby. The full moon was only two days away. I was down on the dock, cleaning and organizing things. While I didn't want to admit it, I was nervous about taking Old Man Lynwood out fishing. I knew his favourite spot was the First Hole, but I was still learning to fish it. On such a big tide, it would be too easy to spend the day tangled. I could see myself floundering around the First Hole at the mercy of the upwelling. You could be sure tales about that kind of performance would make their way around the Seattle Yacht Club.

There was really no upside. I knew Big Jake and Lucky Petersen dreaded taking Old Man Lynwood out to work the First Hole. From the way they told it, no amount of prestige or tips could make up for that much aggravation. I was beginning to regret giving in to Troutbreath so easily.

I stopped scrubbing my floorboards and, as I rested on the handle of my scrub brush, looked out over the bay. All the big yachts were flagged and ablaze with lights. You could hear different parties going on. On the side where the smaller yachts and sailboats were docked, the parties were rowdy and noisy. The parties were a little more serious and subdued at the docks with the sixty-footers and bigger. However, if you paid attention and really listened, you could hear something that was quite new.

It was the sound of other guides doing the same thing I was. It was the sound of long-handled scrub brushes bumping around inside their boats, removing bloodstains and dried herring scales. It sounded like all the guides from the different resorts in Big Bay were down on the docks cleaning up for the day ahead. Of course, Gilly and Heidi, the two guides who had influenced this new attention to cleanliness, were no doubt peacefully in bed, luxuriating in the sleep of those who clean things as they go along.

I knew some of the guides would be taking out their clients before it was even light. That wasn't the way Old Man Lynwood did things. The tide started flooding around nine o'clock. He wanted me to pick him up at 8:30, Troutbreath had informed me, and yes, we would be fishing the First Hole. While I kind of expected to spend the morning there, my internal fishing radar was telling me the derby winner would be caught up at the Log Dump. If it were up to me, I would go trolling along the shoreline past that little spur of rock at the Dump instead of mooching around the First Hole. But I was pretty sure Old Man Lynwood had no use for my humble opinion.

I dutifully arrived at the gas dock at the appointed time of 8:30, where Old Man Lynwood was waiting. He checked his watch and seemed irritated that I was on time. He was one of those guys who was always looking for the mistake. He seemed ready to pounce on any lack of focus or lapse in judgment, always squinting at the world with a pained expression. It was quite the opposite to my sometimes wide-eyed look of terror. I had my sunglasses on, even though the sun had yet to peek from behind the clouds.

No Reserve Box herring for Old Man Lynwood. The 8:30 start time allowed us to visit Burt Asman for some "proper" herring. There would be plenty of time to get over to the First Hole, on the other side of Big Bay, for the start of the tide. When we got to Burt's place, we were greeted by none other than his uncle, Red Asman. His closely cropped red hair and florid complexion gave rise to his nickname. I never did learn his real first name. He always wore grey woollen button-front Stanfields underwear. You could tell today was going to be hot, because he had undone the top button.

It was obvious that Red and Old Man Lynwood had known each other for a long time. Guys like Red were always pleasant to strangers, friendly even. But only people he'd known for a very long time got to know what he really thought. Red and Lynwood picked up their conversation where they had left it the last time.

"How did your fishing trip up the Kenai go? I heard something about a world-record spring salmon. That wasn't you, was it?" Red's eyes twinkled; he already knew the answer.

Old Man Lynwood's pained look intensified. His eyes darted to one side, and he started rubbing the heel of his left hand.

"No, that was Les Anderson, from up there. He got it on the seventeenth of May, just a couple of days before we got there. I saw it in the cooler. Quite the fish, all right! We got a couple of nice ones but nothing that size—ninety-seven pounds and four ounces on a thirty-pound test. Must have been one hell of a fight! I didn't really expect to see one that big so early in the year. We were planning to be back up there end of July, when they are really biting."

The words came pouring out of him. While Lynwood kept on talking, trying to protect himself with a wall of words, Red filled a white bucket with herring, keeping a careful count. You paid for two dozen, you got two dozen. His movements were slow and deliberate, careful to avoid knocking off any of the fish scales. Red knew the flashier and more realistic the bait looked, the better it worked. From the old boathouse, Burt watched the scene between Red and Lynwood play out with some enjoyment.

Red gave Burt most of the money from the herring sales. Red didn't really need the money and Burt more than earned it. He spent many late nights netting and sorting the little fish, getting sore muscles from all the rowing. Burt didn't spend the money on the necessities of life, since he had a comfortable room to sleep in and his aunt did all the cooking. He was very fond of watching movies, though. As there wasn't much to do up here in the winter months, he had acquired an impressive collection of movies on VHS and a good-quality colour TV to watch them on. Any trip to town, he would always return with an armful of the latest releases. A few things signified acceptance in the Stuart Island community, especially if you were going to spend the winter, and an invitation to movie night at Burt's place was one of them.

"Here you go."

Red had finished his careful loading. The herring circled peacefully in the bucket, their scales still intact.

Even though my boat had a built-in herring tank, I knew the bucket was coming with us. My tank was just a metal box, and if we had loaded the herring in there, by now they would have been darting here and there frantically, their noses bloodied by smashing into the walls of the box. The water in it would be filled with scales. There were no scales floating in the white bucket.

As Red handed me the bucket, he continued his conversation with Lynwood. "You almost won the derby last year, eh? How big was the winning fish compared to yours?"

"Mine was twenty-seven and a half pounds. It was winning right up to the end of the day. Then they showed up with forty-two and a half pounds."

"Well, that's what you get for sitting around in the back eddies trying to catch those goddamn little feeder springs. Won't be any left the way you're taking them out." Red had no doubt given this lecture before.

Red, his arms crossed, looked down at me. I could almost detect some sympathy.

"I suppose this is the poor bastard that caught the winning fish last summer." Red nodded in my direction. This was the first time Red had ever acknowledged my existence. I shrugged my shoulders and smiled weakly. I was lost behind the imposing figure of Old Man Lynwood.

"You probably had to pay him double the going rate, just so he'd let you set foot in his boat. Pay them guides that much money, maybe you should goddamn listen to them for once."

Burt appeared as if on cue.

"Take this man's money, Burt." Red waved him in. "And make sure you count it. This guy's always a couple of days late and more than a few pennies short."

Lynwood had to stand there while Burt counted, slowly: "Twenty-five, fifty, seventy-five..."

We all knew Burt was perfectly capable of doing it faster. Lynwood fidgeted, anxious to get going. The flood tide was starting, you could feel it in the air.

Burt was enjoying his moment. Finally, he announced, "It's all there, Uncle Red."

"Thanks, Burt. You put that money in your pocket. I'm sure Mr. Lynwood here has more where that came from." Red turned to Lynwood, who looked like he wanted to say something.

"I thought you wanted to be there for the start of the tide?" Red wasn't giving Lynwood any opportunity to respond. Obviously, he'd had years of practice with the man. Lynwood grunted in reply, and we were on our way.

I managed to arrive at the First Hole without too much water spilling out of the herring bucket. We pulled into the small back eddy to get set up. Lynwood had brought his own rod, a Fenwick 1264 fitted with a big, heavy Penn 49. The first thing he did was to refresh the water for the herring. The care of the herring was almost like a ritual.

I looked on with some interest.

He ignored my cutting board and pulled out one of my paddles. He got it wet, then laid it across his lap. He opened his tackle box, where he kept a razor-sharp knife. He carefully took the knife out of its sheath and set it on the paddle, then leaned over the bucket and watched the herring as they circled. He picked out the plumpest one and deftly scooped it out of the bucket with his left hand. A quick squeeze behind the head killed it and he laid it out on the paddle. He positioned the knife just behind the gills and parallel to the gill plate, at about a thirty-degree angle to the paddle. One swipe and the sharp knife cut the head off cleanly.

Holding the herring in his left hand, he passed the top hook through the high side of the angled cut and pulled the other hook through behind it. He set the two hooks into one side, turning each to bury the top of the hook. Each movement was done very carefully, still keeping as many of the scales in place as possible. When he was finished, only the barbed ends of the hooks poked out of the now ready cut-plug. He dropped the bait over the side of the boat and pulled it through the water. He seemed satisfied with the action of the cut-plug as it rolled.

"That looks pretty good. We can take our position along the rip now." He gestured toward the small line of guide boats that was starting to form.

The tide was moving fast enough by now, the currents beginning to balance. Three boats were already in position. I moved in from the back eddy, turning my stern to the rip that was curling past the point. It was just a matter of backing off on the throttle and letting the current push you toward the edge of the rip line. Once you got close enough, you could adjust the throttle to hold the boat in one place.

With just one fishing rod in use, the boat was much easier to keep in position. Once I had the throttle right, my boat just sat there.

Old Man Lynwood settled into his own little world. He set his own depth and seemed to know every rock and contour below us. His lips moved as he talked soundlessly to himself. He worried and fretted. I had never witnessed anyone work up such a sweat when they were fishing.

The guides and even some of the guests in the other boats all knew who Lynwood was. Some polite greetings and nods of heads were sent in our direction, but they all left us alone.

I didn't have much to do. I found, what with the movement of the water all around, the sound the whirlpools made as they formed behind me, and the occasional cry of the gulls, that fishing with the Old Man, at least so far, was all very peaceful. If I let him do whatever he wanted to do, we were both quite happy. That was probably the very reason Big Jake or Lucky Petersen were as equally unhappy taking him out. Letting a customer get in their boat and do whatever he wanted went against their entire system of belief. I was kind of enjoying it. If I held my boat in the perfect position, life was pretty good.

Unfortunately, life wasn't so good for Old Man Lynwood. Over the next couple of hours, no matter the power of whatever incantations he was mumbling to himself, our perfectly presented bait went completely ignored.

In fact, the First Hole was unnaturally quiet. One of the guides, fighting the whirlpools farther down the lineup of boats, managed to hook a nice coho and left the back eddy to chase it. Apart from that, the rest of us held our positions and waited. Old Man Lynwood's mouth kept moving, soundlessly invoking his incantations.

As the time passed, Lynwood never took his eyes off the tip of his rod. He might ask me to correct the position of the boat slightly, but other than that, we didn't speak. The rod holder he had brought along was clamped to the side of my boat, and he occasionally leaned over it to adjust the depth of his line.

He started to change bait more often. The muttering took on an anxious tone. I noticed him rub the heel of his left hand with his thumb again, a sort of soothing gesture. When I had a chance to look at that spot a little closer, I saw a couple of jagged, nasty-looking scars. He kept returning to them with his right thumb, as if he could still feel some old pain.

A couple of the younger guides gave up and left. They had been fighting the rip at the end of the line, waiting to move up to a better position as people up the line left to play fish, but no one did. Old Man Lynwood watched the rookies leave. I was emboldened to make a suggestion.

"What do you think, Mr. Lynwood?" I broke the hours-long silence. "Shall we give it a try somewhere else?"

"You probably want to go to that log place you young guys are always talking about. What do you call it?"

"The Log Dump."

"Yeah, that's it. The old Log Dump, the place Red Asman set up when he logged that side of the rapids. That was back in the thirties, you know."

I had always wondered why it was called that. There was a vehemence to his tone, as if Lynwood wanted me to know the origins of the name for some reason, but he wasn't expecting to start any conversation.

"No, we can stay here. There should be some big ones moving in here toward the end of the tide."

No big ones ever did move in. We ended up spending six hours, the entire length of the flood tide, bobbing about to no effect. We were the last ones to leave. Of course, when we got back to Troutbreath's weigh-in station, we discovered that the top three fish on the leaderboard all came from the Log Dump.

Old Man Lynwood didn't bother to comment on the obvious. He was surprisingly humble and apologized to me for not getting the winner. I told him I appreciated what I had learned from him, which was quite true. I had watched him get just the right angle on his cuts, looked on as he had checked the roll and adjusted the hooks. He had been doing it since before I was born, and it was like getting a master class.

Strangely enough, after coming in skunked on the day of the derby, I became one of Old Man Lynwood's chosen guides. He told me it was because I didn't talk as much as the others.

LATER THAT NIGHT, there was big excitement on Stuart Island. A stage had been erected on the school field. The band Roots Roundup was laying down a reggae groove that had people dancing. Some television personality was scheduled to present the Stuart Island Community Salmon Derby trophy at intermission. Amid all the excitement, someone had failed to convey some important details to this Television Personality.

When Heidi, the guide whose client had won the derby, got the word that the intermission was about to happen, she reluctantly edged her way to the side of the stage. Her client had asked her to pick up the trophy for him and gave her a very generous tip for doing so. She wasn't thrilled at the idea of being quite so visible in public. People being effusive about something she had accomplished made her feel awkward. But her client wanted to celebrate the event on his own yacht with his family, and she could hardly say no.

As she stood at the base of the steps beside the stage, she found herself next to a white-haired old man. He looked vaguely familiar, but Heidi couldn't place him. He noticed her looking at him and blazed her a grand smile.

"That's right, I'm Ted." He clearly intended that to mean something to her. "I guess we're both waiting for your boyfriend to show up."

Heidi gave him a puzzled smile, but he kept right on talking.

"You must be proud of him. It's quite an accomplishment, or so I'm told. The competition sounds fierce."

It was beginning to dawn on Heidi what this guy must be talking about. He continued to ignore the storm clouds gathering on her face.

"So, are you just visiting for the derby, or do you work here too? One of the cabin girls, perhaps? It must be a great place to get a job, all right."

The Old White-Haired Dude kept talking without interruption. He told Heidi how privileged she was to work at Stuart Island, where her boyfriend was such a successful guide. He let her know what a high opinion he had of this boyfriend in several different ways. Somehow, he managed to keep it going right until it was time to take the stage.

He strode up to the mike with the confidence of a seasoned professional and announced, "Well, I guess our winning guide is off celebrating somewhere. Luckily, his girlfriend is here to accept the trophy for him. How about giving her a big round of applause."

The Old White-Haired Dude reached out to shake Heidi's hand. At that moment, someone fired off the cannon brought in for the evening. Heidi took advantage of the distraction. She smiled, nodded at the man and his outstretched hand, and moved away from the spotlight and toward the exit. She found it almost by instinct.

As she made her way down the dark steps of the stage, she thought about her conversation with Gilly earlier that day. Gilly was right, there was still a long journey waiting for women just trying to be who they were. What had happened up there on that stage was a good example.

While she had just won the Stuart Island Community Salmon Derby on her first attempt, getting the credit would involve a very public discussion with a man who had no grasp of the subject at hand. Sure, she and Gilly might have nicknames, as if they were just one of the other guides, but who knows how long it would take before their nicknames no longer needed to rhyme.

thirteen THE LONG ARM OF THE LAW

THE CANNONS CAME out in force the following day, getting ready for July the Fourth. The signal cannon on the *Song of Joy* was put to good use. Not to be outdone, the Stuart Island Resort unlimbered their old Hudson's Bay cannon. Someone decided it would be a good idea to load it with a couple of rolls of toilet paper. The cannon was situated on a rocky outcropping above the docks, and when it went off, it sprayed shredded toilet paper over most of the boats moored below. I hear they are still finding little wads of it in the superstructure of those boats.

The peak tides were over, and the rapids began to slacken. The water flowing past the back eddies writhed in a somnolent torpor. The summer heat replaced the refreshing winds off the glaciers and hung heavy around the shoulders of the guides. All movement became slow and deliberate. The gunnels and decks of the guide boats were blazing hot to the touch, and the dogfish moved into the back eddies.

The reduced speed of the rapids was not enough to keep the dogfish flushed out of the holes. It became impossible to keep a baited line in the water for more than a few minutes.

Quite often, as soon as a guest stopped letting out line, the unmistakeable chewing signs of a dogfish began. The rod tip bounced lazily, maddeningly, up and down, at least until the razor-sharp plates in the dogfish's mouth sawed the line in two. If you had two guests, their bait would be taken at the same time and, once again, both guests would have to reel up. You'd bait their line as they watched impatiently. Then, when you finally had both lines ready, they would let their lines down again. As soon as they stopped, both lines would start bouncing lazily. In the unrelenting heat on the water, it was enough to make grown men cry.

Some guides stubbornly stuck it out in the holes. Others would give up and run from one place to another. People made the trip over to the other side of the inlet to try trolling; there were still salmon to be caught, even amid the relentless chewing of the dogfish. Our free time was mainly spent tying enough leaders for the next tide.

Meanwhile, events developing to the south, on Read Island, would only add to our misery.

Carl was feeling pleased with things these days. Almost all his growing was done off the property now, but he still used the float house for tinkering on special projects. The new strain of pot he had been working on was finally beginning to show results. As most of his clients were guides, and some of them said pot helped them to find the fish, Carl was quick to see an opportunity. He set about developing a special strain, designed to do just that: to tune the user in to where the salmon might be found.

Carl had been working on the idea for several years. He had tried combinations of as many different strains as he could find. He even tried things like forcing cuttings to root using fish fertilizer. A couple of years had passed since Carl's conversation with Troutbreath one afternoon, when they talked about the oil made from eulachons and all the benefits derived from this magical substance.

At that time, Troutbreath was trying to connect with a source for eulachon. He had met some people from north of Stuart Island who stopped in for gas, and that contact led him to some friends of theirs who still extracted the eulachon oil the old-fashioned way. After netting the fish, they emptied their catch into kelp-lined pits dug in the sand. Left there for several days, the fish would break down, their oil rising to the surface. It would be scooped off and stored in containers.

Carl acquired some of this oil through Troutbreath—he always had something to trade—and started using it to force the pot cuttings instead of the fish fertilizer. Suddenly, it all seemed to fall into place. This new grease-grown strain began to work.

He had taken to calling this new strain "Fish Warp," to distinguish it from his usual offerings. Some of the guides in the know were beginning to ask for it by that name.

"You have any more of that Fish Warp?"

It became a regular request, asked quietly, when no one else was around. Two or three guides in particular would arrive at unusual times, acting furtively. Carl knew they were enjoying an advantage in catching fish, and they didn't want the word to get out. He took it all as a very encouraging sign.

When the RCMP came to visit recently, Carl was upstairs in the float house. He had the place all to himself; Stephanie had gone off to town, running some errands. He was listening to Wes Montgomery and pruning some Fish Warp starter plants. It was a tender operation, and he took great care.

He heard them first, the big twin engines of their inflatable, as they pulled alongside the float house. Carl was not worried. He had no reason to think they were here about his horticultural activities. As he descended his stairs to greet them, he smiled, the great wholehearted smile of an innocent man.

"How can I help you guys this morning?" Carl asked. He was almost face to face with the two officers standing in the big inflatable. "Throw me that rope and I can tie you off so we can talk."

They watched as Carl quickly secured the boat and then they explained the reason for their visit. They showed Carl a picture of a nondescript runabout with an old Johnson outboard.

"We are wondering if you have seen this boat in the area. It has been linked to some thefts from other boats down in Heriot Bay as well as to some break-ins."

Carl considered the photo. It was kind of grainy and slightly out of focus. There were numbers on the side, but they were impossible to read.

"Can't say I have noticed it around. I would remember it for sure. I wish I could be more helpful."

"Hang on to that photo, show it around. Maybe one of your friends might have seen it tied up somewhere. You never know."

"I'll do that. Only too happy to help you guys."

Even to Carl it sounded like he was laying it on a little thick.

"Well, unfortunately, there is one more question I have to ask."

The officer did sound sorry. He reached out a long arm from his boat to where Carl was standing on the dock and plucked something from Carl's beard.

"I don't suppose you could show us where you keep the rest of this? You know I need to ask."

He held up a tiny, perfectly formed, and very distinctive fan of a marijuana leaf.

There really wasn't much Carl could say. He blanched slightly, and the smile of an innocent man turned into the sheepish grin of a known felon. What followed was eminently civilized. Rather than have his new house torn apart, Carl agreed to show them the origins of the leaf in his beard. He also had to show them the cupboard where he kept his cured weed. They were satisfied with that; there was no mention of him selling any of it for a profit. They gave him a summons to appear before the magistrate, which, despite its important-sounding name, looked like a parking ticket.

The police assured Carl that, if he showed up at the time shown on the ticket, the court would be lenient with a first-time offender. They still hoped he would keep an eye out for the boat. It was, after all, in everyone's best interest. With that, they pulled away from the dock.

Carl watched them leave, the ticket clutched securely in his hand so it wouldn't blow away in the wind. He felt he had survived the ordeal relatively unscathed; he felt badly for the guides, though.

When the RCMP left, they took with them all the pot Carl had set aside for Stuart Island. His main crops were far away and untouched, but they wouldn't be ready to use for several more weeks. Carl had to get the word out, but first he was going to shave his beard off. Stephanie was going to be in for some surprises when she got home.

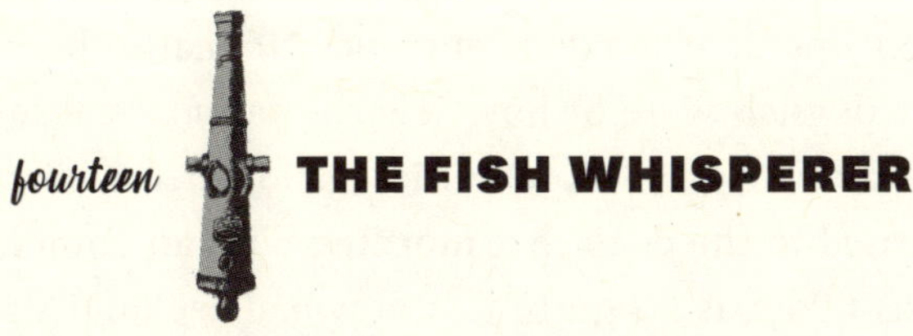

fourteen THE FISH WHISPERER

THE TIDE CONTINUED to slack off. The heat of the summer descended like an invisible fog, and everything that moved became slow and turgid. The current in the main channel flowed past listlessly. The whirlpools yawned open, looked around lazily, then rolled over and went back to sleep. The dogfish continued their relentless work. The guides changed bait, then changed it again. They repeated the same motions, over and over, like dull machinery on autopilot. There was no joy in the fishing holes.

Finding a salmon through all the dogfish was hard enough. The heat made it unbearable. The days became endless. The nights gave some relief but were spent tying more leaders. We spent hours at night attaching two Number Three hooks to twenty-four inches of line, then coiling them up and putting them into a small paper envelope one at a time, repeatedly, night after night. No matter how many were tied, there never seemed to be enough.

Despite Carl's warning about the bust, the guides used his product even more. Their last bags of pot dwindled rapidly. And, as the guides started to run out, they began to return their clients to the docks empty-handed. They were being skunked.

Getting skunked was just one of those things. A rookie guide arriving back at the dock empty-handed was to be expected. As a journeyman guide, I was no stranger to the walk of shame, either. However, some guides, like Big Jake or Lucky Petersen, operated at a different level. No matter how numerous the dogfish were or how few the salmon, those guys could always tease a fish out of hiding. So when Lucky Petersen returned to the dock that morning with an empty fish box, it was taken as a sign of just how bad the dogfish plague had gotten.

By the end of the afternoon tide that same day, a handful of us—me, Lawrence, Heidi, and a couple of the Big Bay rookies—were standing around with Troutbreath having just that conversation.

"I don't know what we can really do about it," Troutbreath said. "I know some people are going way up the inlet and trolling, but you spend most of your time just running from place to place. I know it's a hard slog in the back eddies, but the salmon are still down there."

That, coming from Troutbreath, was what we considered a motivational speech.

"I know Lucky Petersen came in skunked this morning," Troutbreath continued, "but you'll see, he can always find them somewhere. It's almost like he's got some kind of inner fish finder..."

Nobody wanted to say anything as Troutbreath continued to praise the expertise of Lucky Petersen. Or even point out that Lucky Petersen, who had quietly snuck up behind Troutbreath, was standing there empty-handed, listening in. One of the rookies finally nodded in his direction. Troutbreath stopped in mid-sentence.

"He's standing right behind me, isn't he?" Troutbreath said to the rookie. "I have an instinct for these things."

Troutbreath turned around. Lucky stood there with a wide grin on his face.

"Don't let me stop you—I was enjoying that. Unfortunately, for all my expertise, I still came home with an empty fish box."

Troutbreath looked stricken.

"Not you too! What's going on out there? I can't remember the last time you came back empty-handed two straight tides! Well, except for that time when you got cornered by Wet Lenny."

"Oh, it's grim out there, all right. I hope you aren't harassing these rookies too much. It's not all their fault. Carl getting busted down there on Read is affecting all of us."

"What do you mean? How is Carl getting busted affecting you?"

Lucky was beginning to take his private supply of the magical Fish Warp for granted. He had forgotten that Fish Warp was limited to those with the need to know, and Troutbreath hadn't needed to know.

"Hey, I know everybody thinks I'm an old-school, odd-numbers guy, but I'm open to, er... new technologies. All these young guys looking to get my hours—I must keep one step ahead of them, eh?" He had his reputation to maintain, but sharing the joy of Fish Warp seemed like a duty to his fellow guides at this time of need.

"I've even been helping Carl test his latest variety. I think he's calling it Fish Warp. I tell you, a couple of toots of that stuff in the morning and I turn into the Fish Whisperer for the rest of the day. Of course, as these things go, I was on my way down to Read Island to restock when I heard he'd gotten busted. So now I'm out, struggling like the rest of you poor slobs. Well, you know, unless I get lucky, of course."

The twinkle in his eye suggested that could happen anytime now.

Heidi and I were discreet about these kinds of things. We would never mention that a guide like Lucky was having such troubles. With the two rookies being there, however, the news spread around the camp with breathtaking speed.

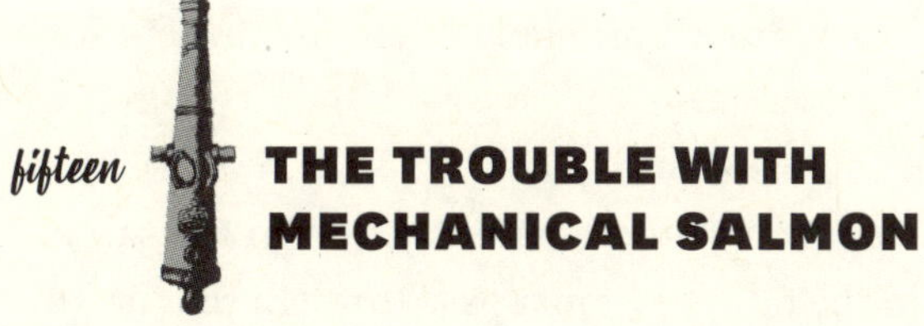

fifteen THE TROUBLE WITH MECHANICAL SALMON

LAWRENCE STOPPED ON the bridge. We were walking over to the pub when something in the water below caught his attention. He stopped to looked at the creek burbling past beneath him.

"Just a sec, you guys. I want to check something out," he said, and scrambled down through the salal.

Without further explanation, Lawrence waded into the creek. The creek emptied into Cordero Channel a short distance past the bridge. It ran all year, but it was shallow in the summer and scarcely lapped the toes of his gumboots. Lawrence made his way carefully over the slippery rocks to a tangle of cedar branches where the creek widened out. I always had assumed they were washed down there in the storms.

Heidi and I stood watching with some interest. Lawrence pulled up a few branches. They were waterlogged but, being cedar, they weren't rotten. The constant flow of cold fresh water had preserved them. He started arranging them. He adjusted the angles of a few. A couple had come loose altogether, and he pushed them back down into the gravel of the creek. In a few minutes, Lawrence had straightened them out and the design became apparent. The branches were now organized into the shape of a funnel, the narrow end pointing up the creek.

Lawrence joined us again on the little bridge.

"What's that for?" asked Heidi.

"It's an old fish trap; it's probably been down there for a long time."

"How is that supposed to trap fish?"

"Well," Lawrence explained patiently, "when the salmon are returning in the fall, they must pass through that narrow end to get up the creek. It's like passing through a funnel. You bring a specially made basket, one that will let the water run through but not the fish. You close off the narrow end of the funnel with the basket. Salmon swims into the basket; you just pick it up and take your fish home for dinner."

"Hard to believe it's that easy. I mean I've got a boat, motors, fishing rods—you're telling me all I really need are some cedar branches?" Heidi was a little incredulous.

"It's got to be the right time of year, of course. And it's maybe not as exciting as playing a fish out of the Second Hole. But yeah, that's the way it works. We can come back in the fall and check it out, but there probably aren't many fish in this creek these days, even during the fall salmon run."

"You said it was old. How long do you think it's been there?"

"Kinda hard to say; those cedar branches will last a long time like that. They've probably been there from before the island was logged, you know, turn of the century or so. You see a lot of these little ones up and down the coast. The ones in the bigger rivers get much more elaborate, with holding pens and stuff. We are in the middle of negotiations with the government, and they want us to prove that we cultivated the land. They have a hard time wrapping their heads around the idea that these kinds of traps are a sign of cultivation."

I had been coming to this island to fish for how many years now and this was the first I learned of this rather sensible way of fishing that had been practiced here for who knows how many generations. The trap seemed simplicity itself, but it was a glimpse into an approach to fishing that was far more sophisticated than jumping into a boat with expensive rods, reels, and lines.

"If you spend the time, you can even control how many fish return and the quality of the ones that make it to spawn. It's like breeding anything; you can select cows for their milk, you can select chickens for how many eggs they lay. Same thing with the salmon passing through the traps. I can make a pretty good argument that this kind of fishing, using traps and weirs and a selective harvest, creates larger runs with better, stronger salmon. But, to say the least, the government is kinda skeptical."

I thought about the last government official I met out in the rapids in his little bouncy-ball boat. The guy had a hard enough time realizing he needed a better boat. I could see that persuading him and others like him that this was a good way to handle fish stocks might be a hard sell.

"So, why aren't the fish returning?" This whole line of discussion was something new for Heidi too, and she had some questions.

"That's one of those questions that has a complicated answer. A little creek like this, though? It is mostly because of the logging back in the day. The gravel beds got clogged with silt and even sawdust."

"Why can't we bring them back? Clean up the gravel and use traps and weirs?"

"Wow, that'd be a big job." Lawrence shook his head sadly, but then looked up with a grin. "It would be easier and cheaper to make mechanical fish, like you guys are doing with the eagles. That's impressive, you know!"

He stopped and paused, staring off into the distance for a minute or two.

"That might work out well. Every fish would be a tyee. You could have different settings on them. If it was the first time your guests had been fishing, you could have a beginner setting. As they get more experience, you could make it more difficult for them, kind of like they do at the ski mountains. You could have a triple black diamond setting, where the fish goes crazy. People would go for that."

You could see Lawrence picturing it in his mind, and the image was growing in my mind too. Finally, he shrugged his shoulders.

"Unless, of course, you want to eat them."

It was the fatal flaw in an otherwise perfect plan.

"Oh, well, you can't use traps and weirs now, you know. The Department of Fisheries and Oceans, in their wisdom, has made it illegal."

"What?"

"Oh yeah, you could report me to the DFO and get me arrested for blocking a salmon habitat."

"But this poor little creek, through no fault of its own, isn't salmon habitat anymore."

"See, I told you it was a complicated question."

We continued our walk. It didn't take long for Lawrence and Heidi to get lost in conversation about other ways his people worked with this land, and it continued on the way to the pub. They both talked with their hands. The more involved they got, the faster they started walking. The path wasn't wide enough for three gesturing people to walk side by side. If I tried walking in front, I was in danger of being run over, or punched, or both at the same time. I dropped behind and followed at a safe distance.

At one point, Lawrence talked about cedar trees and how the people made use of them. The bark was woven and twisted for everything from clothing to ropes and baskets. Long planks could be split off and used for making houses and walkways. Steamed and bent, the planks could be turned into boxes or vessels to cook and serve food. All this could be accomplished without killing the tree. There were many old trees that showed the signs of this kind of harvest.

That did catch my attention—where had I seen such markings? But for the most part, I drifted along behind, caught up in my own thoughts.

sixteen THE BIRD-FEATHERED MEN

BY THE TIME we made it to the pub, Heidi and Lawrence seemed to have forgotten I was following them. Troutbreath was already there, sitting out on the front deck with a couple of guys I didn't recognize. Since Troutbreath was sitting in the full sun, the two guys he was with must have been tourists. Only tourists sat out in the sun. The guides and the dock workers could all be found huddled in the darkest corner, deep inside the pub where no sun ever went.

Heidi and Lawrence disappeared inside, and Troutbreath waved me over to his table.

"Hey, Dave! A couple guys here I want you to meet. This is Lars and Gunnar," said Troutbreath, waving his hand in the direction of the two guys. "Dave here is Ivor's roommate. He helped rescue Einar last season."

I didn't quite know who this Ivor was for a moment. I only had one roommate and he was called Vop. As for someone named Einar, my momentary lack of comprehension stretched out awkwardly. Then for some reason, Stan the Steamer popped into my head. Everything suddenly made sense.

"Um, Einar? Is that the name of the guy Vop, I mean Ivor, found living under the log?" Vop had lent him his Stan Smyl jersey, and we gave him Stan's nickname, since he spoke no English.

"Yes, indeed it is," said the one named Lars. "It was very kind of you two to look after him."

"It's what you do, though, isn't it? I mean, he was half naked, living under that log. That usually doesn't end well."

"Still, you were very generous, and we know Einar appreciated it very much."

"How is he doing, anyway?"

It was an easy question, more of a conversational nicety than really needing to know. The answer had me wishing I had been a little more indifferent.

"Oh, Einar is doing very well these days."

Lars was only too happy to provide details.

"He is just finishing up his art show in Berlin."

"Uh, he had an art show?" Another one of those easy questions that just slipped out, immediately taken as an invitation to elaborate.

"Not just any art show." Lars was getting enthusiastic. "He just had a sold-out show at a very important and influential gallery."

"It was sold out?" I couldn't help myself. "What kind of stuff was he showing?"

"It was very avant-garde."

You could tell Lars was a fan by the way he laid it all out in detail.

"He would get a Berlin newspaper each day of the show and block out the text and photographs in very bright oil pastels. This developed into a series during the exhibit. He also had a series using pieces of wood, like what you might use as firewood. With the same kinds of oil pastels, he traced the grain of the wood. It looked almost like they really were on fire.

"There were a couple of very large pieces, each eight feet by four feet, the size of a full sheet of plywood. He had gone over them in detail too, tracing the wood grain with the pastels. They were quite popular. They got so much interest from several of collectors that the prices went very high."

"High?" I heard my voice croak. "Oh yeah? How high, exactly?"

I did my best to sound disinterested. But my curiosity was getting the best of me. I recalled Stan the Steamer's obsession with my oil pastels last summer, while we waited out a big storm that prevented us from trying to figure out who Stan was and where he came from.

"The collectors started trying to outbid each other. In the end, they both sold for over $100,000 American. Each!"

It was all I could do not to squirt beer out of my nose. The little success I had last summer immediately came to mind. I was so excited about selling two of my paintings for a couple thousand each that I did the happy dance all the way home through the rapids. That little success quickly paled in comparison. One thing about being in the arts, there was always a lesson in humility just lying in wait. A lesson flicking its tail like a cougar, waiting for the right moment to pounce. I cleared my throat ineffectually.

I croaked, "People were willing to spend that much?"

"Oh yes, especially after the interviews."

"There were interviews?"

Damn it, I just couldn't keep my curiosity down.

"Oh yes! He was featured in a couple of art magazines, reviews written by important critics. During the interviews he talked about the future and how it was full of fire, a great conflagration. There was more, but to be honest, I couldn't quite understand what he was on about. He gave the interview in Swedish, but even to me, it sounded like, well, gibberish. The German critics probably couldn't understand him either, but they weren't going to admit it. They decided that he must be some kind of undiscovered genius. I'd say it was based on those reviews that the show did so well. Naturally, we are very happy for him."

"Of course." I had to agree. "I'm sure, um, I'm sure we all are."

"Perhaps you could let Ivor know too."

In something of a daze of disbelief, I left their table and headed inside the pub to find Heidi and Lawrence. A table full of guides and shore staff was already forming, tucked away in the welcome gloom, as far from the sun as possible.

Lawrence was watching the gathering come together with some interest. He waved me over to join him.

"I was waiting in line there to get some beers at the bar," he said as I took my place beside him with my back to the wall. "I couldn't help overhearing that you were talking about Berlin. Does someone from here have some kind of connection to Berlin?"

His voice sounded more quizzical than the question seemed to warrant. Apparently, I wasn't the only trying to decipher life's little intricacies.

"I wouldn't say he was from here, exactly," I replied.

The image of Einar in his Stan Smyl hockey sweater and leather hat still lingered.

"We were talking about this Swedish guy, a friend of theirs. His residence here was temporary, to say the least. Vop found him living under a log. He stayed with us only a couple of days after that, but he managed to leave his mark."

"And what was he doing in Berlin? I mean, why Berlin?"

"He was doing some kind of show, an art show."

Lawrence shook his head.

"It's all so weird," he said, almost to himself. "Ever since I got here."

"What's that?"

There I went, asking questions again.

"Well, no, I don't know if weird is the right word. It's just..." Lawrence usually didn't need to search for words. "It's just—See, there were these nine Bella Coola men. In the late 1800s. They were invited over to Berlin to do shows. They did these shows and lived on display at the Berlin Zoo, dancing and carving masks right alongside the zebras and giraffes. They were there for over a year. They even toured to different cities. They—"

"They were an exhibit in the Berlin Zoo?" I interrupted Lawrence. It had taken a moment for what he just said to sink in.

"I told you it was going to be a little weird. Maybe that is the right word."

"It's already more than a little weird. That's quite the story already." I ordered a beer and turned with interest back to Lawrence.

"I've been looking into their story. There's not much known about exactly what happened. Only three of them we know much about at all. One old photo shows all nine of them in Regalia. Two are wearing beautiful Chilkat blankets over their shoulders. One wears a tunic and leggings with the same pattern as the blankets. Two are wearing large, braided cedar rings around their necks. The guy sitting down in front in the middle is holding an intricately carved ceremonial walking stick. This is the real Regalia, the kind of stuff you see only in museums nowadays.

"Of course, it probably didn't help that the Bella Coola men were in Berlin the same time as Buffalo Bill Cody's Wild West Show. Apparently, these nine Bella Coola didn't look 'Indian' enough. Critics in the Berlin newspapers said they looked more Japanese than anything else. The people promoting the zoo hired a photographer, who was told to make these guys look more 'Indian.' So the photographer decided they needed feathers in their hair, like the guys in the Buffalo Bill show. The only problem was that the zoo had no eagles, only pheasants. The photographer didn't seem bothered by the difference."

"Seriously?"

"Seriously. He used feathers from pheasants. So, along with displaying all these rare and precious West Coast artifacts, these poor guys have pheasant feathers sticking out of their heads! I mean, honestly, it looks kinda ridiculous."

"I can only imagine."

"You know the really weird thing, though?"

"That's not weird enough already?"

"It gets even more wonderfully convoluted. There were other pictures in the collection I was looking through. They showed Buffalo Bill's people, all dressed in their regalia—eagle feathers, buckskins. You know, I guess looking the way Indians are supposed to. But if you look closely, you could see most of the women and even some of the men were wearing dentalium shells. The only place those could have come from was the west coast of British Columbia, around the islands here. Some of my ancestors might even have been the ones that gathered them. The shells were traded all up and down the coast and into the interior."

Lawrence was in his stride, and I was a willing audience. I didn't know what dentalium shells looked like, so he explained that they are long, narrow cones, usually with a slight bend, mostly white in colour. They look a bit like tusks but are actually the shells of molluscs that hang out about ten to fifteen feet below the low-tide mark.

"Gathering these shells was quite the procedure. You had to have specially made poles with kind of these fingers on the end. You dip the pole into the water, leaning over the edge of your canoe, then the fingers grab the shells from the mud and lift them out. Of course, it's not as easy as it sounds. Those shells end up being quite valuable.

"The people that traded in them had marks tattooed on the insides of their arms like a ruler. The longer the shells were the more they were worth. Some of Buffalo Bill's people were showing off a great deal of wealth, given the number of dentalium shells they displayed. Meanwhile, the people who harvested that wealth were, you know, dressed up in pheasant feathers. They didn't look Indian enough."

"Didn't I watch something similar take place with you and a couple of guests on the gas dock? I got the impression you were a disappointment to them."

"Yeah, that was an interesting session with those two guys." Lawrence smiled and shook his head. "So you can see why, when I heard you talking about Berlin, the hair on the back of my neck stood up."

"Another coincidence? What do you think it means?"

"Who knows, eh? I don't want to read too much into any of it. A guy can drive himself crazy. Sometimes a coincidence is just a coincidence. Of course, it's all going to come back and haunt me when I try to get to sleep tonight. Between stuff like that or dreaming about having your head cut off like a herring..."

"You have that one too? Vop is especially tortured by the herring dream, for some reason."

"How do you guys get any rest?"

"Honestly, we are all basically sleep deprived. You learn to live with it."

LATER THAT NIGHT, Vop and I were sitting at the table tying leaders, as usual.

"So, Vop, when you and Carol used the cabin for a couple of fishing trips last fall, you guys burned the last of our firewood, right? Including the stuff Stan the Steamer decorated? And used his newspapers as starter?"

"Yeah. Why do you ask?"

"Hm." I was already beginning to feel a little heartbroken. I was doing the best I could not to start adding up the price of last fall's heating bill, when Stan the Steamer had been drawing on our firewood.

"Whatever happened to that piece of plywood? The one we gave him to make a bed—the one he decorated with the oil pastels, same as he did the firewood?"

"You know, I forgot to tell you. In all the excitement that happened with my engine coming off the boat and all, it slipped my mind. I used it to help launch my boat."

"Uh, you what?"

"It was one of my better moments. I couldn't get the boat to move over the beach all by myself, and then I remembered that old piece of plywood. I put it down with the painted side up and the boat just skidded along it like it was greased. Which, in a way, with all that oil pastel, it kind of was,"

Vop finished a leader with a flourish, as if to add an exclamation mark to his story.

"That oil pastel did leave kind of a mess on the bottom of my boat, but it's kept the barnacles away."

"And the piece of plywood?"

"By the time I was finished with it was kind of wrecked. I broke it up and it's still behind the boatshed, waiting to get tossed. Why, did you need it?"

"Oh no, I was just thinking about it today. You know, maybe the living room could use some brightening."

"There wasn't much left of it. Maybe one piece that still has some colour left. We could put that up...?"

"No," I sighed. "Sounds like it's past its usefulness. Let's just leave it behind the boatshed, shall we?"

I tried not to show any disappointment. I didn't have the heart to tell Vop what I knew. He seemed so pleased with his resourcefulness. We both lapsed into silence and concentrated on the task at hand, tying leaders. The next day would bring so many dogfish.

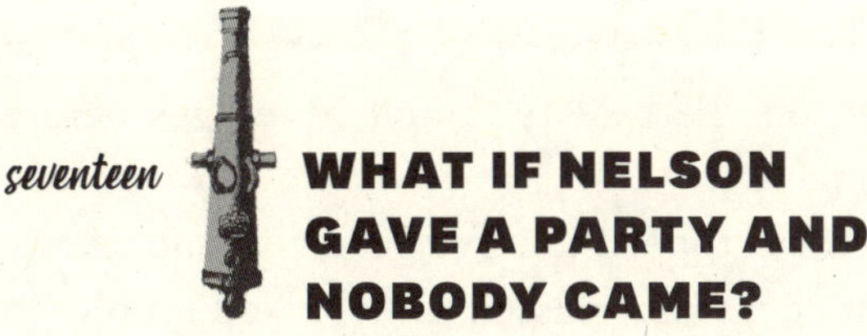

seventeen WHAT IF NELSON GAVE A PARTY AND NOBODY CAME?

OWNING A RESORT wasn't really a money-making proposition for Herbert. It was more about having a place to tie up his boat. Nelson and Gilly were a little more invested, though. They were paid a modest amount as caretakers, but their real income came from guiding the guests of the visiting boats. Unlike some of the other resort owners in the area, Nelson was dependent on the yacht traffic.

Now that Herbert had offered them a bigger share in the business, Nelson, chagrined by the toaster incident, felt he still had to prove himself. He stood at the top of his dock and looked down at all the empty berths. The small tides, and the accompanying onslaught of dogfish, were not the only reason the yachts were headed elsewhere. Word of the world-record salmon caught at Kenai quickly spread along the entire coast. Alaska was suddenly the place to be.

Nelson and Gilly knew they had to do something. Their beginning-of-the-year party had been so popular, despite the loss of the toaster, that they thought a similar event, tailored more for an upscale crowd, might be worth trying.

They both went into town, leaving the resort looking like some kind of ghost ship. They stopped in at the local newspaper office, where they bought a large advertising space to promote the party. They got some posters printed up at the same time and left them on every dock in the area. Finally, they stocked up on the best food and beverages before heading back home.

On the way, they stopped to leave posters at the resorts and government docks they passed. Gilly talked it up with people on the marine radio.

They had given themselves a couple of days to prepare. They went on an expedition to collect clams and mussels and to catch some ling cod, and they pulled some salmon out of the freezer. There wasn't enough time to waste trying to catch any, but anyway, the real star of the barbecue was going to be Grade A Vancouver Island beef.

What with the advertising and food and drink, it had all cost a bit of money. Nelson and Gilly were sure it was going to pay off.

The day arrived, and they waited for the boats filled with guests to pull into the docks. The potatoes were washed and ready, the salads were waiting to be tossed together, the steaks were resting in the walk-in cooler. Nelson and Gilly hoped most of the boats would be docked by the end of the tide in the afternoon, but slack water came and went and the docks were still empty.

They both remained optimistic as the time passed. That optimism persisted until darkness had fallen.

"I guess I should start wrapping the steaks so we can put them in the freezer." Gilly was the first one to break the long silence.

"Can't believe we didn't get anybody," said Nelson, more to himself than Gilly. "I figured worst case would be only three or four boats, but nobody at all?"

"You know, we are going to have to explain this to Herbert. Most of the expenses will come out of the resort expense account. Maybe Herbert will let us pay it off over time."

"I'm not ready to have that conversation tonight," Nelson sighed.

Nelson might have had a better night's sleep if he had known what he and Gilly had set in motion. His worst-case scenario of three or four boats would have been a sad little cook-out indeed. But with not a single boat, in a place that drank exclusivity like coffee, the two of them had inadvertently hosted the most exclusive barbecue Stuart Island had ever known. Everyone was going to want a piece of it.

The first inkling of what was to come arrived at the next morning's slack tide. A lone cruiser pulled into the dock. Nelson went down to help them dock, and—well, he couldn't quite believe what he was hearing.

"Say, we heard about your party last night. Sorry we couldn't make it. It sounds like we missed a great time," the skipper said as he threw the tie-up lines to Nelson.

"You heard about the party?" Nelson needed to clarify this for his own sake.

The skipper's wife continued breathlessly, "People were talking about it on the marine radio. You must have enjoyed yourselves!"

"It was an evening I'm not going to forget for a long time," Nelson said frankly. He was basically telling the truth.

"Well, we hope you guys have another one soon!"

With the boat securely docked, Nelson rejoined Gilly. She had kept an eye on the proceedings and heard enough to be curious.

“What were they saying about the party?”

“Apparently, we are the talk of the marine radio waves. But, you know, it’s just the Samuelsons; they are a little out of touch at the best of times. I still need to let Herbert know what happened.”

It didn’t take long for Nelson to raise Herbert on the lodge radio. Gilly listened in while she worked in the kitchen.

“Herbert? Nelson here. Just wanted to touch base with you about the party we had. We used some of the resort funds to pay for the advertising and all the food and drinks. I’m feeling kind of bad we didn’t run it past you first. Over.”

“Are you kidding? People at the yacht club here in Seattle are already talking about it and nothing else! Sounds like a great time. I only wish I had been there. Don’t worry about the money—that’s what it’s there for. You guys are doing a great job. We can talk some more about my business proposal when I see you. Over.” Nelson was quite speechless; even Herbert was caught up in the excitement. Nelson wasn’t going to try to interrupt and correct the gossip. “Oh, and there’s something I wanted to let you know about. Bob Fiske has the cougar mounted and ready for the lodge. It’s all crated up. It won’t fit into the plane, though. Doug Perkins and his wife are bringing their boat up. The cougar is going to arrive with them. Uh, over.”

“Hey, that’s great news. Over,” said Nelson. He hoped “great news” was vague enough to cover the party as well.

“I’ll fly up to meet them. They probably won’t get there for four or five days. Over and out.”

There was a metallic click followed by a little bit of feedback, and Herbert was gone. Nelson looked at the phone for a minute. The party was the talk of the yacht club in Seattle!

Nelson continued to be incredulous as he heard the stories coming back to him. Each one was more fantastic than the last. Another batch of boats arrived on the afternoon tide, and Nelson listened quietly to the latest embellishments.

He soon realized that Dinah Shore played a main role in most of those embellishments, which was understandable. She was a well-known singer, actress, and television personality. It was also well-known that she often stayed at the resort and was a favourite guest. It seemed reasonable that she would have shown up and taken over the kitchen. She had, after all, recently published a cookbook. Everyone knew one famous dish from it: Mr. Whipple's Seafood Filet Gumbo. Nelson was apparently a genius to have had her cook that as the featured main course for the party.

Nelson heard that story more than once. People were sad to have missed such a legendary feast. In the course of each retelling, when the name of the singer and television host doing the cooking came up, people would hesitate. Women would shrug their shoulders, and men would briefly turn their eyes away, but none of them could stop themselves.

"After all, if you were given the choice," they would say, "why would you dine afloat when you can Dinah Shore?"

There were other stories. One going the rounds claimed that all the cannons on Stuart Island were arranged on the front deck of the resort, firing broadsides. Considering the logistics of moving the large and unwieldy Hudson's Bay cannon up from the south end of the island, that one sounded a little far-fetched, even to me.

eighteen MATING HABITS OF A VANCOUVER ISLAND COUGAR

NELSON AND GILLY basked in the glory of their incredibly successful party for some time. I stopped by to check the mail a few days later, and people down on the docks were still lamenting having missed out. I had heard the Dinah Shore story more than enough times. I made my way past everyone without making eye contact.

I noted that Hebert's floatplane was tied up at the dock. It always made me approach the resort with caution. Things could suddenly lurch out of control whenever he was around.

When I arrived at the front desk, Nelson was trying to explain the Canadian postal and monetary system to Mrs. Samuelson.

"Yes, Mrs. Samuelson, I know. The package is just going to your niece in Seattle for her birthday," said Nelson. I always admired Nelson's studied patience. "And you're right, it isn't very far at all, but I do need to see what's in the package; the postal service has rules about this. As the postmaster here, I need to inspect the contents of all international parcels. Yes, it does seem silly, but Canada and the United States are two separate countries, and there is a border between them. That nice man in the blue janitor's uniform you talked to, that wasn't just a safety inspection he did on your boat..."

I knew the situation well enough to settle in for a long wait. I rested against the wall. Beside me, Herbert sat in the alcove, and I couldn't help but overhear him talking on the resort's radio telephone.

"No, no, I just have to say I am very grateful. You guys got the job done faster than I could possibly have expected and shipped it up here in good time. You know, I had to jump the line at the tanners. That's going to cost me a couple of fishing trips for the guys in front of me, but it was all worth it! I mean, why own a fishing resort if you can't use it to your advantage occasionally? Right, Bob?

"Now, we really wanted to get this beauty back up here so people can appreciate your work. I know people will be asking me for your business card. But, well, I guess you know what I'm going to say next..."

He released his talk button for a moment.

"What's that? Yeah, I talked to the Holdersen brothers before I called you. They told me the same thing. No, no, I know you called them too and tried to work together on this. You and the Holdersens are the best there are. That's why I came to you in the first place. I mean, not only are you the best cat guy in the whole Tri-States, but everybody also says you're a real straight shooter. I trust you, of course I do. But isn't there something you can do? I wanted it to be up on its hind legs snarling. You know, real scary. But..."

And here Herbert paused for a bit, his finger lingering on the talk button to prevent hearing the other person talk.

"But it's... it's... You would think the damn thing is smiling. Over."

Mrs. Samuelson finally left, probably not much wiser for all of Nelson's explanations. It was my turn for the mail. I couldn't help but ask Nelson what Herbert was on about.

"It's just us right now. Let's go into the main living room and have a look. It's hard to put it into words. You must see it for yourself."

Herbert had cleaned off some shelves along the back wall facing the big picture window. In their place was a beautiful glass case with accent lighting. Inside it was the old cat, presented in a natural setting, like an exhibit in a museum of natural history. He was posed standing on his hind legs, front paws outstretched. However, it was not the snarling, hungry beast Herbert had imagined. It was doing more than smiling.

"What do you think?" Nelson asked after giving me a long time to take it all in.

"I am imagining what I see?"

"No, it's not just you. In fact, if it was up to Gilly, there would be a plaque that said '*Felis concolor vancouverensis*: Mating habits of.'"

"*Vancouverensis*?"

"Yeah, it's a subspecies of cougar. Apparently its coat is slightly darker than the mainland ones. Like so many of us here, it must have come from Campbell River."

I had to admit this Vancouver Island cougar didn't look fierce.

"Anyway, we are being careful how we talk about this when Herbert's around. We aren't even calling it a smile!"

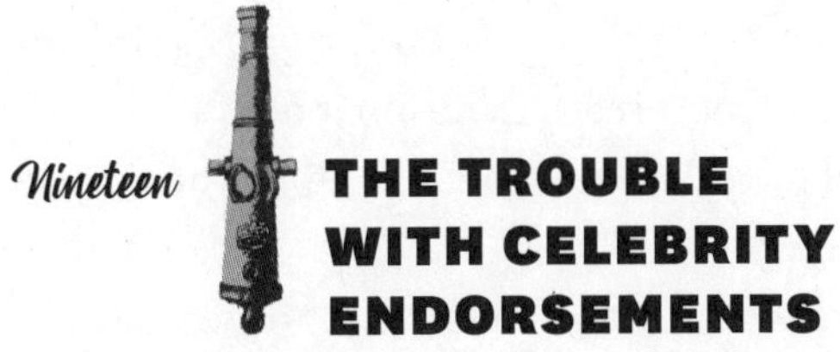

Nineteen THE TROUBLE WITH CELEBRITY ENDORSEMENTS

MY NEXT STOP that day was the gas dock. When I got there, I found Carl surrounded by a group of anxious guides.

"Well, yeah, I put up a mirror so I can see myself before I leave the house now," he was saying as I joined them.

"What happens next?"

"It's already happened."

"Don't you have to go to trial or something?"

"I pleaded guilty. I mean, I was. The judge gave me a stern lecture, warned me never to appear in his court again, and fined me one hundred dollars."

"Now what are you going to do? I mean, if you can't grow anymore."

"Who says I'm going to stop growing? It's what I do."

"Yeah, but aren't you afraid of showing up in that guy's court again?"

"First of all, I have it on pretty good authority that he is going to be retiring soon. And even if he wasn't, now that word is out that Lucky Petersen uses my pot, I not going to be able to keep up with the demand. I don't want to do it, but I might have to talk with the growers I know on Cortes, see if they can help. We might be able to make some kind of arrangement.

"But anyway, with all that court stuff out of the way, I managed to make it to one of my stashes that the RCMP didn't find. I don't have much, but it should keep you guys going for a while. I've given it to Troutbreath to ration it out."

"How come he gets to hang onto it?" one of the rookie guides asked truculently.

"Because he's Troutbreath—do you need any other reason?"

Carl's look was a warning, and the guide, not wanting to risk getting on Carl's bad side, shrugged his shoulders and kept quiet.

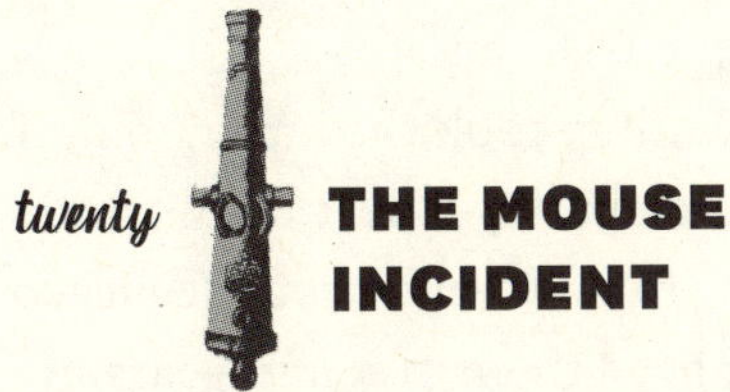

twenty THE MOUSE INCIDENT

CAROL AND VOP hadn't seen much of each other. While Vop was busy guiding, she was throwing all her energy into their new home on Cortes. She was hard at work putting in flower beds and raised beds for vegetables. The walls and floors of the log cabin sparkled, all freshly oiled or varnished. When Vop compared what he was doing—fishing with his guests while enjoying a cool beverage, catching some sun—to how Carol occupied her time... well, he had to do something to right the balance.

Vop took some time to make a few arrangements. One of his regular yacht-owning clients had their float plane moored at Big Bay. Vop traded some fishing time for some flying time, which he had done with them in the past. Carol was alerted through the usually complicated method of a radio telephone call. She did manage, through all the static and bad signals, to ascertain she needed to be on the float plane dock at Whaletown at a particular time a couple of days later, ready to visit Stuart Island.

Vop got busy around the cabin he and I shared while we were guiding. When he wasn't on the water, he was cleaning the floors and windows. He tidied up the place, even arranging the old Alfred Hitchcock magazines into some semblance of order on the bookshelves. The kitchen got a going over, too, but he wasn't going to cook. Vop planned a special meal, to be prepared by Baba. Vop haggled with Troutbreath over one of the prized bottles of wine in his collection.

The day Carol was to arrive, Vop took the afternoon off. The cabin was already clean and sparkly. But it wasn't quite good enough yet for the evening he had envisioned. He picked wildflowers and tastefully arranged them in canning jars. He dug out the emergency candles and used Troutbreath's empty wine bottles as candleholders. I must admit, by the time he was finished, the old cabin looked like a warm and inviting place. Finally satisfied, Vop went over to see Baba and pick up the freshly cooked dinner. It was all packaged up and ready; all Vop had to do was serve it. Baba refused any payment from Vop.

"It is what we do for our friends," he said, when Vop tried to insist.

Carol arrived like a celebrity. The float plane landed in the bay and taxied majestically over to our dock. I was there to greet it and help Carol off the plane. I carried her bags up to the house while Vop shouted greetings through the front window. Carol was impressed with how well the cabin looked. The wildflowers even made it smell nice. She was obviously ready to take a break from hard work and enjoy a lovely meal and some relaxing time with Vop.

I made my excuse to head over to the Wheelhouse Pub to have dinner with friends and left them alone.

The food Baba had made took the evening to a completely higher level. Vop and Carol savoured the meal, chatting and catching up. There was much to discuss, especially about the work she was doing; for instance, how great the stones of the living room fireplace looked after a good scrub. They talked about plans for the new house. They floated the idea of adding a guest house and where it could sit for the best views.

Finally, there was a lull in the conversation. They both continued to enjoy every morsel Baba had prepared for them. It was a quiet evening. The forest was still, with just the sound of the rapids far off in the distance. In that quiet, Vop detected some very subtle sounds. He immediately knew what it was. Vop also immediately knew what was about to unfold, and there was nothing he could do about it.

It was the sound of tiny feet, with even smaller toenails, scrabbling across a piece of cardboard. Vop had finally gotten tired of sharing his cheese. He had taken a five-gallon white plastic tub—like the one Lucky Petersen used for herring—and fashioned a lid for it out of cardboard, with a balanced piece that swung open and shut like a trap door. He made a ramp out of the cardboard and laid a trail of peanut butter leading to the trap door. Up until a few days ago, the mouse would have landed harmlessly on the bottom.

As Vop listened in the quiet evening, he could track exactly what was happening on the bucket. The scrabble of little feet following the peanut butter stopped at the trap door. Vop heard it swing open, and with a gentle "splouch," the little mouse hit water—the six inches of water Vop had recently added in a pique of exasperation. The swishing of little feet swimming was clearly discernible, for a moment. Then the scrabbling began again. This time, those tiny feet were scrabbling at the slick, plastic sides of the bucket as the mouse tried, desperately, to find a way out.

Vop silently poked at his food. The struggles of the little mouse were all he could hear. The poor thing thrashed along the side of the bucket, getting more and more frantic. Vop could only hope that Carol wouldn't notice. He started to say something, anything to cover the sounds. Before he could get out his first word, however, the tiny creature realized the true awfulness of its situation. From a small feast of peanut butter, it found itself unexpectedly and suddenly in a hopeless life and death situation. The terror of its predicament finally became too much.

It started to scream.

It was a shrill scream of absolute terror, with gruff undertones of injustice. A scream that echoed down through generations of such small creatures subjected to brutal, unthinking indifference. A scream that recognized the prospect of death. A cold, miserable death in an inescapable bucket of water. It was a scream of desperate, forlorn hopelessness.

Vop did not look up from his plate. The screaming got louder, growing until it filled the cabin. It was surprising how much sound such a tiny body could produce. Vop continued poking at his meal, his own sense of panic growing too. Carol finally said something.

"Oh, Vop. Don't tell me you put water in the bucket trap!"

Vop felt the mood of the evening lurch dramatically out of his control. "I tried catch and release, but the damn thing kept coming back for my cheese," he mumbled.

"How much of your precious cheese could a little mouse like that possibly eat?"

The screaming got even louder.

"It left footprints," said Vop weakly.

"Ivor Vopnstrom! You're not going to just sit there and let that poor creature drown, are you?'

Vop stood up from the table like a marionette being pulled on invisible strings. There was nothing else to be done. He walked over and retrieved the bucket, with its wretched passenger, from under the sink.

"I'll, uh, I'll go down to the beach and let it go, then?"

Carol sat in stony silence. Vop stood there holding the bucket, feeling that it was his turn to be forlorn. The creature had screamed itself out by now. From inside the bucket there emanated only the tiny sounds of splashing and a pathetic whimper.

"Or maybe in the woods behind the boathouse. The little guy would like it there..." Vop's voice trailed off.

The stony silence continued.

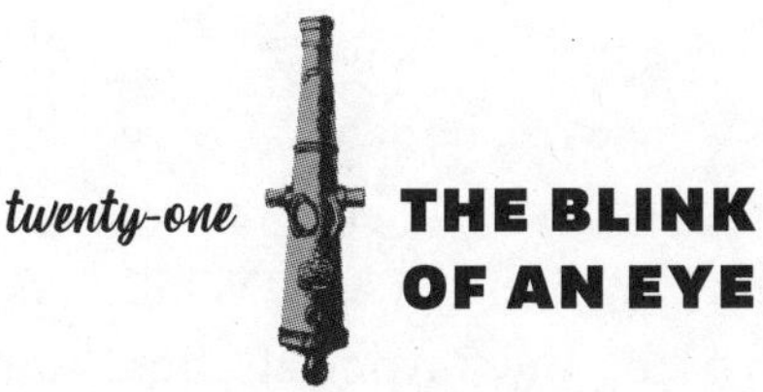

twenty-one THE BLINK OF AN EYE

IT WAS HARD to say why exactly, but over the next few days more fish began showing up on the cleaning tables. The more practically minded could point to the tides getting stronger again, flushing the dogfish out of the back eddies and pushing the feed of salmon inward. However, many guides saw that it obviously coincided with Carl's arrival and the sudden availability of his newest strain, which everyone was now calling Fish Warp.

Then Lucky Petersen hooked into a forty-six-pound tyee out of the First Hole. There was no question in his mind what the reason was. Suddenly, the little stash Carl had left for Troutbreath became very small and very important indeed.

LARS AND GUNNAR were still in the area on their new boat, the *Pagan*. They were always up for a little time-bending. When Troutbreath approached them looking for a little respite from the demands of being Dock Boy, and now Chief Supplier of Fish Warp, they were more than enthusiastic. They had been working on some new theories and wanted to put them to the test.

There was much folklore about being able to travel through time between stones carved with certain petroglyphs. What had happened to Einar—Einar with the sudden gift for making a lot of money from his art—was especially intriguing. He had appeared, completely naked, in a location completely different from where the stones were when he had started, which resulted in his having to find refuge under a log. Having gone into the future certainly might have been part of it. While Lars and Gunnar were in no hurry to send anyone else into the future, they wondered if the device they had created to power the stones might also be used to send someone to a different location. The ability to choose the physical location to which you were sending people back in time might have its uses.

They explained all this to Troutbreath. On top of the usual dangers of time travel were some unknowns. Whether they could bring the time traveller back was one of them. Troutbreath didn't take long to make up his mind. What with moorage for boats, moorage for float planes, keeping up with the demand for the well-used tide charts in his personal collection, explaining to people how to keep their boats floating, and, in the middle of the night, both keeping the Reserve Box topped up with herring and supplying his guides with Fish Warp, Troutbreath appreciated the diversion.

Troutbreath knew he wasn't going to find any down time, at least not in his present timeline. In addition to his supporting roles for the fishing guides, he had used the small tides to do some diving around the dock and now had a full inventory of rods, reels, sunglasses, fishing lures, and variously expensive boat parts dropped over the side during repairs. These all had to be cleaned, identified, entered into his inventory book, and tagged with prices. Troutbreath was finding the role of entrepreneur was more work than he ever expected. The idea of getting lost in time had its appeal.

He headed off to the petroglyph stones with Lars and Gunnar. Waiting for their equipment to warm up, Lars and Gunnar gave Troutbreath one last chance to change his mind. He appreciated their concerns, but he had an inexplicable trust in their abilities. Perhaps Troutbreath had been around enough incompetence over the years that, when he finally found conscientious people going about their craft, he was willing to trust them. They were going to try sending him to a spot on the south end of Stuart Island. They thought that a clearing at the top of a bluff overlooking the water would be a relatively safe site to send him to.

"There are no trees for you materialize inside, no matter what date you arrive there, since it's bedrock," they explained confidently.

"Let's give it a go," said Troutbreath, trying to sound equally self-assured.

With that, he stepped onto the stone and disappeared from 1985.

HE MATERIALIZED SAFELY, and his new location looked familiar: it was indeed the south end of Stuart. That was something that always caught him by surprise. No matter what the timeline was, even when Error 18 took him back deeper in time than usual, as it had in past journeys, the scene was always the same: the same rocks, the same trees, the same landscape he could see in 1985.

Once he made this realization, it seemed perfectly obvious, and he smiled at himself. What else did he expect, really? A couple of hundred years might seem like a long time, but for the rocks and even the trees around him, it was no time at all. It was the blink of an eye.

It wasn't just the sights, either. The sounds were the same, too. The rapids in the distance, the grunt of seals, the crying of the gulls, the shrill whicker of the eagles. Well, okay, these were actual eagles, not mechanical ones. The noises the mechanical ones made were almost the same, but hearing the real eagles was rather startling.

There was another, more familiar sound as well. Someone on the water behind him was having a party on their boat.

Troutbreath could hear all the usual sounds of camaraderie—laughter, loud voices, dishes clinking—but there was something else, too. He couldn't quite identify it. It was very familiar, but perhaps unexpected and out of context. He cocked his head to one side as if that would help him.

Then someone yelled, "Home!"

"Home?" thought Troutbreath. That was kind of a random thing to be yelling. If that was a question, he hardly knew where or even when home was anymore.

Before Troutbreath could get too nostalgic about home, however, the same voice yelled, "Shot your gun!"

Troutbreath didn't need to hear any more. Someone behind him was loading a cannon. This wasn't Tydesco Chemical's middle management doing the loading either. It was being done by a well-trained crew, with a gun captain shouting the correct sequence of commands according to British Naval drill. Each precise command was followed by scrapping and rasping sounds in a precise order. Taken all together, though, with a party going on in the background, it still sounded like a Fourth of July at Big Bay.

Troutbreath, his head still cocked quizzically to one side, turned around. It was a good thing his familiarity with cannon fire prepared him for happened next.

twenty-two HOW CORDERO CHANNEL GOT ITS NAME

JOSÉ CARDERO TOOK a deep breath of the fresh air blowing across the deck. It was one of the things he loved about this part of the world. The air that poured down off the mountains all around him carried with it a hint of the snow that lingered, even into the summer months. Taking a breath here was as refreshing as taking a bite of a cold, crisp apple.

It was such a contrast to the fetid stink belowdecks. The *Mexicana* had proven to be a thoroughly wretched vessel. She was newly built in San Blas at a cost of more than ten thousand pesos! For all that money, much more work had to be done to make her seaworthy. The ship had spent weeks longer than expected being outfitted and strengthened in the shipyards at Acapulco.

Even then, her mainmast broke on the voyage north, and they had barely made it to Quadra's outpost at Nootka Sound, a couple of months ago. There, she was immediately beached, and it became apparent that more repairs were needed; the mainmast and foremast both had to be replaced. The hull was not even sealed properly, which may have accounted for all the pumping the crew had to do to keep the bilges dry.

That constant dampness also explained the foul and mildewy air belowdecks. Captain Vancouver himself, who had a tour of the *Mexicana*, was appalled and outspoken about the conditions he observed. After all, the ship was barely forty-five feet in length, yet home to twenty-one officers, servants, crew—and José, the so-called ship's artist. Vancouver was a very taciturn man, and some said his attention to the health of his crews was mostly due to his own self-interest. He had served with Bligh when they were both lieutenants under Captain Cook. The news of mutiny aboard the *Bounty* was still being addressed by the Admiralty when Vancouver had left London. You could be sure he had no interest in being set adrift in a ship's boat by an angry crew. Yet, even so, his concern seemed genuine.

As José took in his surroundings, he still was trying to clear his head of the chaos of being aboard the *Mexicana* on their surveying trip from Nootka to the middle of these Discovery Islands. Here was such an array of sights and sounds for the beholder. José loved the twisted trees, bent into shape by the winter gales. The shoreline was hard granite and dropped off precipitously into the depths. While Vancouver, who called the area Desolation Sound, might have missed the tame surroundings of his home at King's Lynn, José enjoyed the ruggedness. To his artist's eye, each tree had its own personality.

He listened to the strange whistling cry of the white-headed eagles, the ever-present screeching of the gulls, and the singular sound of the ravens. The *Mexicana* was tied off close enough to shore that he could make out some of the birds on land.

He was happy to be back despite the somewhat difficult conditions, conditions that were the stark opposite to his first voyage. On that expedition, he was on a much larger ship, one that had all the considerations and room he needed. He had had a proper workspace, with drafting tables that weren't also used to serve food. Most importantly, his job really had been ship's artist; other people attended to the mapmaking duties.

He could hear the festivities to celebrate the completion of their survey work getting underway on the English ship tied off a short distance away. All the crews were gathered on the deck of Vancouver's ship, the *Discovery*. Even this close in to the shore, the bottom of the channel dropped off quickly. It was so deep and rocky here that anchors were mostly useless. It was more effective to run a line to shore and tie off to one of the many large trees.

For the last several weeks, the Spanish survey expedition, led by Galiano on the *Sutil* along with Valdés in charge of the *Mexicana*, had accompanied Vancouver on the *Discovery* and *Chatham*, commanded by Broughton. They had shared the survey work, charting the inland sea between the mainland and Quadra and Vancouver Islands. Now that that popinjay, Johnstone, had finally sent over his notes, this last island in what they were calling the Discovery Chain could be added to the charts—José's job.

José had excused himself from the celebratory visit to the *Discovery* with the pretense of finishing those charts. Of course, what he really wanted was the peace and quiet to finish the portrait that was consuming him.

HE KEPT RELIVING the night he first met her, the subject of his latest drawing. When the *Sutil* and *Mexicana* were finally seaworthy enough to leave Nootka Sound, they headed south. Before entering the Strait of Juan de Fuca, to start their exploration of what turned out to be the inland sea, they put in at the small Spanish outpost at Neah Bay. The Spanish were considering the suitability of moving their main settlement there, depending on the outcome of negotiations with the British over Nootka. José couldn't help but wonder by whose authority all these pompous announcements were being made.

At Neah Bay, they met someone whose every movement and gesture was filled with effortless authority, a Makah Chief named Tetaku. Tetaku had a strong, fierce countenance, and his very presence left most of the junior officers unnerved and in awe. They tended to huddle together, not unlike prey animals seeking the protection of a herd. His eyes seemed to pierce right through them. His clothing was made of cedar bark and the fur of animals. He was always barefoot but did not seem to notice the barnacles or sharp mussel shells on the beaches. He was nimble and completely at ease in a boat. It was all quite wild and caught everyone's imagination.

He was invited on board the Spanish ships by Galiano. Tetaku took up the offer with some alacrity. One of the junior officers, who stood out from the rest and had also served with José on the previous voyage, had learned enough of the language used on the coast to be quite useful. With his help, Galiano and Tetaku discussed the *Mexicana* in some detail. Tetaku was very curious about its construction, and he seemed quite taken with the room available. He indicated he was envious of the amount of cargo it could carry.

A couple of days later, as the Spanish were getting ready to leave, Tetaku reappeared and let them know that he too was planning a trip into the Strait of Juan de Fuca. Valdés suggested he accompany them on the *Mexicana*. Apparently, Tetaku had anticipated the invitation. He waved over a couple of canoes that were piled high with woven cedar baskets, cedar chests, and bentwood boxes. He was quite delighted to unload all these goods on to the *Mexicana*, with the help, of course, of the *Mexicana*'s crew.

This great assortment of things was intended, as it turned out, to be used for trading. The baskets held smoked clams, dried fish and other kinds of meats, seashells of various kinds, whale oil, and things made from whalebone. José saw whalebone tools for weaving and preparing hides. Tetaku was as much of a designated trader as he was a Chief.

They learned there were several villages tucked into the sheltered parts of this coast, all connected by established trading routes and familial links. The trails leading away from the village were wide and well established, where perhaps whole companies of men could walk.

Tetaku was most concerned about the welfare of the goodly number of smoked clams in his cargo. He conveyed to the *Mexicana*'s crew that they were somewhat perishable and the result of much work in harvesting and preparation. José had noticed raised beds holding clams along the beach near the village, so the word "harvest" seemed appropriate. Tetaku intended to trade them for the oil of a certain small fish called eulachon. They were like herring, but smaller in size and prized for their oil. He gave José a small taste, and it was like nothing else José had ever experienced. It seemed to embody the essence of this place, from the crisp mountain air to the smell of seaweed in the sun and the beaches at low tide.

Tetaku stayed close to Valdés, observing the way he directed the operation of the ship. Valdés, in turn, followed Tetaku's suggestions. He directed the *Mexicana* north to what the crew knew as Puerto de Cordóva, or, as the English called it, Esquimalt Harbour. It was a relatively easy and safe journey across the strait to the large, well-established village there. And fortunately, a quick one, for with all the extra cargo on board, the crew could hardly move about. Tetaku assured them a valuable supply of fresh water was available in Esquimalt. He seemed connected with that village in some way.

The village was a cluster of longhouses fashioned out of cedar planks. They all were facing the beach, with many canoes pulled up onto the sand in front. Carvings of various magical creatures leapt out of the facades of each longhouse. The trunks of tall trees had been carved and erected in front of them. They were not unlike the carvings José had seen in Tlingit villages, and he knew they identified the different clans that lived in each longhouse.

Shortly after the Spanish made anchor, two of the large cedar dugouts that had been following them from Neah Bay arrived. A woman was in command of each canoe, each with a team of paddlers. Both canoes were laden with even more trade goods, including two young dogs asleep on top of the woven cedar bags. Although treated as pets, José learned their fur was used for weaving.

Of the two women, one was slightly older and had a small baby with her. Tetaku immediately went to her, and from the way he doted on her and the baby, it was clear she was his wife. The younger woman was quickly surrounded by the people arriving on the beach from the longhouses. She was dressed in a manner very similar to theirs; it was easy to assume she was originally from this village, though she was undoubtedly Tetaku's second wife. The young officer who had been serving as interpreter was able to confirm this. While Tetaku treated her with a great deal of deference, she seemed more like a sister to him than a wife. In Spain, José was familiar with marriage arrangements that bound different families. This place seemed no different.

That night, the officers and José were invited on shore to share the evening meal. Over the course of the extended meal, José marvelled at the bounty of food that was served in bentwood cedar boxes. Large fire pits had been dug into the beach to roast venison, salmon, and other items. The seafood included the smoked clams and dried and smoked salmon, as well as a fresh flatfish very similar to halibut. There was one unusual offering: the inner bark from some kind of evergreen tree had been pressed into cakes, placed in a specially carved bowl, and doused with the prized eulachon oil. The revelers took turns breaking off small pieces with their fingers. It was treated like some kind of delicacy.

This eulachon oil itself was a prized commodity. Served in delicately carved bowls, it was always in easy reach. Each bowl had a special ladle made from the horn of a mountain goat. The Spanish men had been seated in a place of respect, next to one of the largest bowls of oil. José watched all night as people dipped the ladles into the thick liquid and dripped the precious oil over their food.

José tried to thank his hosts for providing such a feast. First they looked puzzled, then, with some laughter, they assured José this was a normal evening's meal. There was a feast planned to celebrate Tetaku's arrival, but that would take a few days to organize properly. José was assured this would be much more bountiful with dances and ceremonies. He was sad to tell them that by that time, the *Mexicana* would have left to continue its explorations.

Tetaku and the two women sat across from José. Tetaku was received with great respect, not unlike that given to a Spanish noble. But the respect seemed to be about something other than nobility. Even a minor Spanish lord would never associate himself with something so beneath him as trade. Tetaku, on the other hand, was showing off a great array of the goods he had brought with him, and he took great delight in sharing with those at the table.

At one point in the evening, another important-looking individual approached Tetaku with a finely woven basket filled with white shells. They were cylindrical and wider at one end, like a flared tube, and very hard and fluted, like the finest Italian porcelain. Tetaku allowed José to inspect one; it felt heavy and substantial in his hand, like a precious object. They were very difficult to harvest and thus rare. José thought they were being used as currency.

Tetaku had some unusual marks on the inside of his left arm, a series of evenly spaced dots. José realized they were tattoos carefully placed with some purpose. Tetaku used the dots like a scale for measuring the length of a shell. The longer ones gave him more satisfaction. Sometimes he would stop to admire an especially excellent one. When he was satisfied, he put the basket on the ground beside him. Tetaku spent the rest of the night with his older wife, eating and making a continuous fuss over the baby she carried with her.

José couldn't take his eyes off the younger of Tetaku's wives. Her eyes danced and sparkled as she took in the excitement around her. Her hair was loose and shining; she had no use for powders or false curls. Her complexion had no need of artifice of any kind, no rouge or beauty marks. She wore a long white cape, a warm and luxurious fabric woven very finely. Draped over her shoulders and arms, it settled like clouds, accentuating the curves of her body .

She seemed quite happy to be back on familiar territory. Many people approached to pay her respect and make conversation over the course of the evening. The small dogs played at her feet. According to the young translator, the two dogs were welcome gifts and the source of the fine wool used to make the cape.

Her necklaces and earrings caught and reflected the firelight, many made from the precious white shell tubes. The inner parts of another kind of shell showed a liquid pearlescence, deep blue, green, and a rich purple, the rival of any precious stone. José came to understand that to have such adornment was a sign of her high status and great wealth.

At the meal, Valdés announced to Tetaku that, as he was a very important Chief, it would be fitting for José to create portraits of him and the two women. By the time José got to Stuart Island, he had already completed a portrait of Tetaku as well as one of his first wife. It was the portrait of Tetaku's second wife that was proving to be a struggle.

She was beautiful; he couldn't help but notice. He was finding that fact to be quite distracting. She sat for her portrait on several occasions before the *Mexicana* finally left Puerto de Cordóva. They had spent more time trying to converse with each other than he had spent drawing. Despite having no common language, they managed to communicate sufficiently, mostly with hand gestures and facial expressions. She had learned how to say his name, but hers, with its liveliness and guttural sounds, was beyond José's linguistic abilities.

"SO, THIS BE your first time sailing in these parts?"

The harsh voice startled José out of his reverie. He had almost forgotten the man was there. The English had sent some poor wretch named Moffat over in the *Discovery*'s smallest rowboat to deliver the notes and surveys for the final charts. José immediately took pity on the man and invited him on board. Moffat was now perched on a stool opposite José, who spread his art supplies across the bench beside him in the wide stern of the *Mexicana*.

Moffat had already complained about his lot in life, expressing great disappointment in missing out on the party and his extra ration of rum. José had decided to give the man a treat. If he was to miss out on the party, José wanted to make it up to him.

José had put that the extra time spent in Acapulco to good use by acquiring some of the special hemp they grew there. The introduction of hemp to Mexico went all the way back to 1545 and Hernán Cortés. The Spanish navy used the hemp to produce fibre for ropes and ships rigging, and when José was there, extensive fields of it flourished around Acapulco. In the mountains above the harbour, the combination of soil, sunshine, and the gentle ocean breeze made for ideal growing conditions. Over time, the resin content of the plants had increased and the growers employed patient selection practices, choosing the best and most potent specimens to propagate further.

But the Spanish were also aware of the "medicinal" benefits of this plant. José had secured an abundant supply of this mountain-grown "*marijuana*," the Mexican slang for the plant. They also called it "*mota*" ("speck"), perhaps a reference to how little of it was needed to obtain the desired effect.

José was also very happy to find in Acapulco a place that sold the Spanish-made Pay-Pay tobacco paper. He now laid a sheet of it on the ship's bench and began to prepare it for cutting, first following the ritual of folding and creating creases along which to cut. Moffat watched his progress closely.

José replied to Moffat's curiosity as he worked. "No, I was here just last year, but much farther north, in the land of the Tlingit People. We were sent by the King of Spain to search for a northwest passage said to be found at sixty degrees north latitude. We sailed directly there."

"And you was ship's artist then?"

"Actually, I was a cabin boy. I was a servant to Señor Galiano, who at that time was serving under Captain Malaspina. I had some talent with drawing, and Señor Galiano was kind enough to encourage me to continue. While we were being outfitted in Acapulco for that first trip, we took on Señor Tomás de Suría, who had proper training in rendering and making charts from Spain. I learned a great deal from him, at least enough to be kept on, and here I am."

He went on to tell Moffat proudly that now, at the venerable age of twenty-six, he, Don José Antonio Cardero, was listed on the manifest of the *Mexicana* as ship's artist, declared such by none other than the Viceroy of New Spain, the Count of Revillagigedo. They doubled his salary.

"But they neglected to mention their intention to increase my misery one-hundred-fold. Sadly, I am an ink-stained wretch, amidst all this beauty, stuck in a dank hold in charge of drawing maps."

Moffat nodded. He was only too familiar with being stuck in jobs no one else wanted.

"You must be doing something right. I 'ear tell they're going ta name a little stretch of water after you."

José began cutting, adding a few extra papers to use later.

"So I understand, although it seems to me these places have enough names already," replied José. "I hear it was much to the displeasure of Master Johnstone. It seems he was very reluctant to give up even a tiny sliver of water from the strait named after him. I will consider myself most fortunate if they spell my name correctly whenever they add it to our map."

"Master Johnstone, 'e's a proper fop that one, 'im and 'is shiny black shoes. What sliver of water is it?"

"On the north side of the rapids is a narrow channel that runs along the mainland. You know that unusual small passage that opens to it? At low tide it is like a small creek. I have just finished drawing it on the chart."

twenty-three LA SEGUNDA MUJER DE TETAKU

JOSÉ SAT IN companionable silence with Moffat, continuing to prepare their smokes. He spoke again, more to himself than the man sitting across from him.

"There is a clearing just above that small turbulent passage, a flat spot on a small piece of land surrounded by the rocky cliffs and water. It would be the perfect place for a hacienda, a refuge from the insanity that is beginning to engulf our world back home. A man could enjoy a wonderfully peaceful, undisturbed life there. *Una vida pacifica.*"

José smiled at his small play on words. A wonderful and peaceful life indeed, especially in the company of one of these women of the islands. He tried not to think of the woman his imagination conjured. It would not do to have such thoughts about a woman, never mind one connected to such a powerful Chief. However, a man could do well with such a companion. There was something truly refined, even royal, about her manner. At the same time, she could scramble about the canoes as sure-footed as any of the men in her command. In her own quiet way, she was very much in command.

"Out 'ere in the middle of this forsaken wilderness? I wouldn't even be able ta sleep 'ere. All those savages in that village around the shore in Vancouver's Bay."

José winced. Yet another place now bore the name of the English commander. Before long, even the wild beasts would carry his name. José was finding it all to be a little too much.

"These people are hardly savages."

José was afraid of giving his thoughts away, but he couldn't stop himself from speaking of his experiences with Tetaku and his people.

"We couldn't have done this survey without their help. Tetaku welcomed us and, as he is a Chief, having him on board showed others up and down the coast how to follow his lead."

José was sure Moffat knew the extent to which his "savages" had assisted all the surveyors. But Moffat was one of those men who felt uncomfortable associating with people from a different culture. After all, a proper gentleman didn't go about barefoot!

"Without them we might have all perished in these 'canals de remolinos,' or whirlpools, as you call them. I believe they even towed your Master Johnstone through some of the worst of it, using ropes from the shore. They have done as much or even more than any civilized people would. We should be thankful for them being here. If you want to consider savagery, there is talk among the officers of a new device invented by the French—a machine to cut people's heads off! It is said to be faster and more humane, as if that is a virtue."

"I suppose, now you say it like that, you might be right. I've never eaten as good anywhere else I've been."

"Earlier you spoke with some wonder," continued José, "about the place settings on Captain Quadra's table. Well, we might have brought the silverware, but it is these local people who keep it filled with food. They are keeping us safe and well fed; what more can you ask from anyone?"

"But the way they just come and go without a 'by your leave'!"

Moffat wasn't prepared to concede much.

"If you ask me, there's something wrong going on 'ere. It's not right. Why, just the other day, we was finishing up the survey of this island. I was helping 'Is Lordship Johnstone relieve 'isself on shore, like. Well, if one of them savages didn't just appear before my very eyes, just like that. And 'e was naked as the day 'e was born. 'Is Lordship tried to talk to 'im. You know, see if 'e needed any assistance. He babbled some kind of meaningless jabber. Master Johnstone looked away to call for a blanket, and just as sudden, this fellow disappears. I said naught about it to 'Is Lordship, mind you. A man could get sent off ta Bedlam for less."

José let the man chatter on. He didn't really pay that much attention; after all, there was no one more superstitious than an English sailor. He started to roll the herbs inside his special paper.

"So..." Moffat finished his speech and quickly moved on to more important matters. "Why don't you use a clay pipe instead of that chart paper? That 'ud get you flogged on the *Chatham*, it would."

"Those clay pipes are fine for tobacco, but they clog up quickly and become useless. I brought this paper with my own coin. It's especially made for smoking tobacco or my fresh marijuana herb, which has travelled with me all the way from Acapulco," José patiently explained.

Moffat looked at José's preparations with new respect. "I've heard of this kind of thing afore. I 'ad mates on other ships sailing for that East India Company. 'Gangee,' or some such, I think is what they called it. I've never tried it meself."

Moffat was very curious, but he had some reservations. "What's it going to do to me?"

"Quit worrying. You are going to enjoy it."

"How'm I supposed ta know it's working?"

"*Pronto lo sabras*—you will know soon enough."

"It's not goin' ta start me acting odd then, is it?"

"You mean like seeing people suddenly appear and then disappear?"

"'Ere now, that was real, that was!" It seemed the tale of Lieutenant Johnstone's run-in with another of the naked men on this very shore not too long ago had made the rounds of all the surveying ships.

Moffat sat facing José in the stern, his back to the island, petulantly replaying again his version of the naked man's appearance.

José filled the Pay-Pay paper with precision, taking pride in his work, but also taking time to admire the scenery, a bare cliff overlooking the rocky shoreline. The *Mexicana*, tethered by the bow to the land rather than anchored, the water being so deep there, was the closest to shore of the four ships. Suddenly, a naked man appeared atop the cliff, his back to José. The man stood still for a few moments, looking around him. He cocked his head to one side, as if listening to something familiar.

José heard it too, above the chatter of the Englishman. A gun crew on the *Discovery* was unlimbering one of their four-pounders. The well-practised team would soon have it loaded and ready to fire. As José smoothed out the herb into a neat line along one end of the paper, keeping his eye on the naked man, he could envision the crew loading the cannon with powder and tamping it down.

He rolled the herb-filled paper between his fingers and listened to the commands emanating from the *Discovery*, which sat farther back from the shore. The ship's gun crew added wadding and a cannonball, ramming it home. José licked the edge of paper roll lightly and gave it a twist, then reached a long sulphur match into the banked fire of the cook's oven. He sheltered the flame in his cupped hands and held the match to one end of the roll.

He took a couple of puffs to make sure it was burning properly, then handed it to Moffat. Moffat held it very gingerly and took a small puff without inhaling.

"Take a long draw and hold the smoke in your lungs," said José, trying to be helpful.

José noticed the naked man turn around and look out over the water. His mouth moved oddly as if he were talking to himself. Even from where José sat watching him, it was clear that the man seemed to be lost in wonder at the sight before him.

All this was taking place behind Moffat, who shrugged his shoulders and took a long drag, then closed his eyes and held his breath. There was a moment's pause. José heard the gunport on the *Discovery* open and the squeak of pulleys running the gun out on its wooden wheels. One final shouted order, then the naked man threw himself onto the ground.

Boom! Four pounds of red-hot cast iron ripped through the space where the man had been standing. With a great splintering crash, it buried itself into one of the sturdy fir trees that grew out of the rocks behind him.

The *Mexicana* rattled from the force of the sudden explosion. The sound of the blast rolled across the water and reverberated off the surrounding mountains. Moffat opened his eyes. He looked in wonder at José's cigarillo that he held in his hand.

As José watched, the naked man, lying face down on the ground, seemed to vanish into the air. One moment he was lying on the ground, the next moment he was simply gone.

As the echoes of cannon fire subsided, the two men exchanged a quick glance. They both burst into laughter at the same time, throwing their heads back in abandonment. They basked in the great release such laughter gave them.

twenty-four SCARS

TROUTBREATH LOOKED IN wonder at the sight before him. It was Error 18 all over again. This time, instead of just one of *Discovery*'s rowboats, though, he was looking at a flotilla. The ships closest to shore, two forty-six-foot unarmed schooners floating serenely on the calm water, flew the Spanish flag.

The two ships flying the English ensign were twice the size of the Spanish ships and anchored that much farther out. He could read the name *Discovery* on the one that had swung broadside to the shore, right in front of Troutbreath.

It took a moment for Troutbreath to take it all in. The noises which had alerted him continued. He watched, mesmerized by the scene in front of him.

The now familiar voice shouted, "Run out the gun!"

A small square porthole opened on the side of the *Discovery* and the snout of a ship's gun poked through it. As Troutbreath's luck would have it, it was pointed right at him. The cannon was winched out as far as it could go, the squeaking of its carriage wheels followed by a shouted command that carried easily across the dead-calm water.

"Fire!"

Now, the English Navy didn't believe in firing blanks, and the roll of toilet paper was yet to be invented. This was a properly loaded four-pounder cannon of His Majesty's Royal Navy. Fortunately, Troutbreath realized what was about to happen. He instinctively threw himself onto the ground. He landed hard on the rocks; a tree root punched him in the ribs.

"Oof! What the hell is it with these people?" he heard himself say out loud.

An incredibly ferocious *boom!* shook the air. He felt the cannonball pass above him, through the space he had just occupied. The sound clanged inside his head and left his ears ringing.

He felt the shockwave shake him loose in time and the telltale pull of the stones in the pit of his stomach. How the time had changed was the question.

Troutbreath carefully raised his head and looked around. The ships were gone.

His ribs were quite sore, and the wind had been knocked out of him. He was in no hurry to stand. As he lay quietly and listened, he could detect none of the modern sounds we take so much for granted: the sound of float planes and motorboats, the distinctive whiny buzzing of a chainsaw. The sun was a little colder; perhaps it was earlier in the day. His senses told him he had changed to another time, but he had no idea when that might be.

When Troutbreath got his breath back and felt safe from further cannon fire, he stood up. Looking around gave him no hint of the year. He decided the best thing was to return to the stones. The deer trail he knew from his own time was still easy to follow. It was not a long walk, but it was slow going in his bare feet. The trail was strewn with sharp pieces of gravel, thorns, and broken, jagged branches.

If he was back to the fifties, his usual time to visit, he hoped to find his stash of clothing. It was turning into another pleasant summer's day. Finding something to wear was more about not being seen in his present state of undress than wanting to keep warm.

Carefully watching every step, Troutbreath had plenty of time to consider his present circumstances. In particular, his next entry in Lars and Gunnar's time traveller's logbook. His arrangement with Lars and Gunnar included helping them understand and analyze his time travel experiences. While he hadn't materialized inside one of the trees, he did materialize in the middle of a live cannon-fire exercise directed at the trees. As far as he knew, it was the first time someone had ever fired a cannon at Stuart Island. It was an inaugural event of sorts. *And of course, the damn cannon was pointed right at me,* thought Troutbreath. He wasn't sure about the wording, but Lars and Gunnar would hear about it.

They also needed to hear what happens to a time traveller when a small cannonball passes too close. Troutbreath couldn't really blame them, though. That wasn't their fault. Time just had it in for him. It made Troutbreath think about alternatives. He had been warned about the future, but really, how much worse could it be?

As Troutbreath slowly walked the trail taking him back to Big Bay, his mind wandered. Once he had explained to Lars and Gunnar what it felt like to be subjected to cannon fire from one of His Majesty's ships, he could share some more abstract musings. It seemed to Troutbreath that he kept returning to certain time periods, as if time had its own set of vibrations. The confluence of these vibrations created these nodes to which he returned. For some reason, 1792 seemed significant.

Troutbreath knew enough history to recall that in 1792, there was a truce between the Spanish and the English, enough to enable them to chart the inland sea together. He also knew that the Battle of Trafalgar loomed just a few short years away. At least one person present at Stuart Island in 1792 would be killed there. Galiano, by then a brigadier and in command of the seventy-six-gun ship *Bahama*, was killed by a cannonball on that day, the twenty-first of October, 1805. His body was consigned to the sea. Troutbreath couldn't imagine what that battle must have been like or how it must have felt to die in that manner, although he now had some small inkling.

Troutbreath was relieved when the trail finally made its turn downhill into Big Bay. He quickly reached a cabin, on the site of Vop's summer home, but the house looked too clean. The paint was still fresh, and there were no cracks in the windows. This must be long before the cabin started melting back into the forest. Even before Troutbreath started to slip in and out of time, he had researched the history of Stuart Island. He always wanted to be prepared for the questions people expected him to answer. Judging from the photographs he had seen, he suspected he had landed sometime in the 1930s.

The hollow tree stump, his hiding hole for clothing, was empty, which seemed to confirm his assumptions. Keeping to the bushes behind the house, he worked his way around the side to the boathouse, hoping to find at least some rain gear or even a tarp he could wear. A pair of oil-stained overalls, even with someone else's name on them, would be very comforting right now. As he got closer to the building, he could hear voices. Troutbreath eased his way along until he could peek through the side windows.

Inside was a beautiful white rowboat, bathed in the rays of the morning sun filtering through the windows. The boat looked lean and agile, very easy to row and designed for fishing the back eddies, in a time before outboards took over. It was on a carriage built for the wooden tracks running from the boathouse down to the water. Those tracks would make launching the boat easy. A line ran out of sight from the carriage, probably to a winch for hauling the rowboat back up from the beach. In Troutbreath's future, these tracks were just decayed pieces of the wood that still poked out of the sand; now he understood what they used to be.

The voices were coming from two people hunched down near the stern of the boat. Troutbreath couldn't see them properly, but it sounded like a father and son, the father trying to teach the son something. Troutbreath didn't normally like to eavesdrop on people, but the phrase "cut-plug" immediately got his attention. Using a cut-plug was a method of fishing that he thought had begun much later than the 1930s.

Even though he was naked and his chest was bruised, and he wanted to get back to his own time, Troutbreath had to listen in. The evolution of the cut-plug was a hotly debated subject.

The two sat on wooden crates, between them a white enamelled bucket filled with water. The father balanced a paddle on his lap, then reached into the bucket and splashed some water onto the paddle. He put his hand back in and came out with a herring. A quick pinch behind the head and he was able to lay the now dead fish onto the paddle. With a sharp knife, he cut the head off at a blunt angle. He explained how that precise angle would give the bait a slow roll that the big salmon seemed to prefer.

Troutbreath was making mental notes. He marvelled at the size of the herring they were using. They were huge!

"I want to go over this one more time, so you really get it," said the father.

"I can do it. You've shown me hundreds of times—I can do it!"

"The derby starts at the beginning of the flood. We have time to practise it some more. You want to win this, don't you? Why, it's the first derby the Community Association has ever hosted. Think about being the first one to get your name on the trophy!"

The boy carefully picked the herring up off the paddle. The man gestured impatiently.

"Goddamn it, you've got to get your hands wet first, or you'll take off all the scales. The more scales you leave on the bait, the better it looks to the salmon. How many times do I have to tell you that?" The father sounded irritated.

The boy put the herring back down. He wiped his hands on his jeans, looking a little flustered. He dipped his hands into the water and carefully picked up the herring again. He reached for the top hook of the leader that was lying on the paddle.

"Okay, that will have to do. Now put that top hook into the low side next to the backbone and poke it through to the high side. Just the way I showed you. Try not to take any more scales off, for pity's sake! Now grab the point of the hook carefully and pull it through, and pull the other hook along with it." The boy faltered, his small fingers fumbling with the thin metal and slippery fish. His nervousness in front of his father only made him try to grip the cut-plug tighter, making things worse.

"Now drop the top hook and grab the shank of the other one and pull it carefully all the way through. Goddamn it, your little brother can already do this. What the hell is wrong with you? No, not like that—here, let me show you again!"

"I can do it myself," the young boy yelled and snatched his hand away from his father's grasp. As he did so, the line must have gotten caught on something. The leader pulled tight and both hooks, filed razor sharp, sank deep into the palm of the boy's hand. He let out a squeal of pain.

"Jesus Christ!" the father yelled. "What the hell? What a stupid thing to do! Damn it, don't try to pull them out. They're buried past the barbs and pulling only makes it worse!"

The father quickly cut the leader line to stop it pulling the hooks deeper.

"Look at what you've done."

The father held his son's hand up and inspected the wound.

"That tide is going to start soon. You go get your little brother and tell him to bring all his leaders too."

"It's okay. It doesn't hurt," said the boy, holding back his tears.

"Don't be stupid. You can't row the whole tide with your hand like this. No, you go get your brother. Tell him to bring along all the leaders he's been tying. He's going out instead of you. Then get your mom to walk you over to see Mrs. Asman. She has been up here for years and has plenty of experience taking those hooks out. Go do that right now."

Troutbreath had to move farther back into the woods so they wouldn't see him when they emerged from the boathouse. He found a sunny spot and settled in to watch from a distance. The boy ran up to the house, his hand held out in front of him.

Soon, a smaller boy ran out of the house, a tackle box in hand. His arms and legs flailed with joy as he sped around to the front of the boathouse.

The mother, her son trudging along after her, emerged and quickly set off to see Mrs. Asman. Troutbreath had heard stories about old Mrs. Asman, the matriarch of the Asman clan. There was no doubt she was the right person to visit in this situation, with her experience raising sons in such a remote place. However, Troutbreath was quite happy he wasn't the one trudging off to see her, head down and nursing a very sore left hand. Those hooks had to come out, but Mrs. Asman didn't believe in painkillers and was known to be quite liberal with the iodine.

The real show started not long after the two of them disappeared into the forest. The bow of the rowboat emerged out of the boathouse. Its white paint gleamed in the sunshine. The varnish on the sheer strake and gunwales sparkled. The father and the younger boy guided it from either side. They didn't have to do much to help it coast down the launch track; it was more about keeping this thoroughbred from being too eager to get into the water.

The younger brother was grinning broadly and seemed full of youthful enthusiasm. He dashed into the water to keep the boat from scraping on any rocks, not caring how wet he got. He held the boat steady while his father climbed in. Then, while the man rowed out to the dock, the boy ran back to the boathouse and winched the now empty carriage back inside. He picked up the small tackle box and ran back down to join his father.

Troutbreath could guess the contents of that tackle box, but he would have loved a peek inside. A small herring crib floated on the inside of the dock, and the boy carefully scooped some more herring into their bucket before deftly climbing into the boat. His father made some last-minute adjustments to the seating positions and then the two of them rowed off to the First Hole to catch the start of the flood.

As much as Troutbreath wanted to witness the inaugural Stuart Island Community Salmon Derby, he was tired, a little sore, and most important of all, he was starving. He was more than ready to get back to his own time and Uncle Baba's kitchen. Troutbreath knew finding his way back to the stones was going to be difficult.

He found some paint-spattered overalls in a heap in a corner of the boathouse. Troutbreath was pretty sure no one was going to miss them. They were as much for protection against being scratched and stabbed by the salal branches and thimbleberry thorns as they were for modesty.

Troutbreath returned through the woods along the familiar trails he used to go to the lake or out to the Near Side viewpoint, which were clearly deer tracks. He used the mountains around Stuart Island to triangulate his direction. Once he got closer, he could recognize some of the landmark rocks and trees. Then, finally, he was close enough to feel the familiar pull.

"AI-YI-YI! You eat lunch less than an hour ago! How can you eat so much food and still be so skinny?"

Troutbreath was happily seated at his special table in Baba's kitchen. He thought about the question. Since lunch, he had been transported back to the wrong timeline, dodged cannon fire, been dislodged into a time he had never visited before, walked back to Big Bay in his bare feet, and watched a young version of Old Man Lynwood experiencing a formative lesson. How do you even begin to explain that to someone?

"I have to tow some herring boxes at slack," Troutbreath explained between bites. "I'm probably going to miss supper. Gotta fill up when I can."

twenty-five THE SOLO TYEE

THE LONG, SLOW streak of fishing was coming to an end. Once more, there was action in the fishing holes. To make it even more interesting, the late summer run of northern coho also began. I had a last-minute cancellation and, since my time was already paid for, I decided to catch a fish or two of my own. I knew of a business in Campbell River that made lox. The idea of some cold, smoked fish to take home for the winter was always appealing, but I would need to get lucky for that to happen. I needed to catch a fish big enough to make it worthwhile.

By the time I arrived, the Second Hole was already a busy place. I cut in at the top of the back eddy and twisted my throttle right down. The momentum of the boat carried me along. I wanted to slip in quietly and not disturb the people with actual paying customers. I let my boat drift into the small float put there for just this purpose. I could tie off while I got my line ready. I took my time and watched the action unfolding in the fishing hole.

People were chasing coho wherever I looked. You could see the silver flash of fish jumping and the chaos that ensued. To increase my chances of catching one, I chose a smaller, bright-coloured herring. I cut the head off at a sharper angle to get a fast, tight spin and sank just one hook up into the cavity against the backbone. Then I started my small motor and untied my boat. The tide caught me almost as soon as I left.

I must admit, an extra pair of eyes in the fishing hole could be quite useful, especially when it got like this. Sometimes clients have their uses. I used the small fishing motor to pick my way out into the Second Hole, perching on the edge of my seat and trying to see in all directions at once. I felt my boat get caught by the stronger currents, and I let them take me. It was important to ride the current, let it determine where your boat went.

I dropped my bait in the water as the water pushed me back to the top of the hole. I turned my bow out toward the main channel and let the current push me once more. I was in a good position to start my first drift down the outside of the Second Hole.

Five minutes later, I was headed back to the small dock. I'd cut my line to save a guest in one of the other boats from losing a nice coho. I had to restring my rod and replace my weight and leaders, but I felt some urgency to get back out there—the bite was unpredictable and could stop at any moment.

After threading the line through the eyes on the rod, I replaced the weight, main leader line, and the leader that held the hook. Then I had to tie the swivels and knots correctly. As urgent as the moment seemed, there was always time to do it properly. I was equally careful to select the right herring and cutting it so it would spin quickly, the way the coho loved it.

Finally, everything was ready, and I untied again. Two other boats had pulled up to the small dock, their guides furiously retying their lines as I left. These boats each had two customers, who all impatiently observed their guides' progress.

I was even more careful as I approached the hole. A rookie in close was playing two coho, and he obviously hadn't had that opportunity before. I gave him a wide berth.

I let Big Jake go past playing another double-header. He was the last person I wanted to tangle with in the Second Hole. He practically owned the place. I could hear him start shouting instructions to the rookie. They ended up trying to occupy the same patch of water. Both Big Jake and the rookie stood up and began passing rods over and under and from boat to boat, trying to undo a macramé fishing line. I silently wished them the best of luck.

I picked my spot, a small opening in the crowd. I got my line down, but some instinct made me look up at the First Hole. Lyle Donovan was headed right toward me. His customer was standing up in the boat, a look of supreme concentration on his face. They had obviously picked up a monster out of the First Hole. The fish, with them in tow, was headed right for me.

The Donovans, like Red Asman, had been at Stuart Island for years, running one of the first resorts in Big Bay. I had the opportunity to guide for them on a couple of occasions, which I took as a rare privilege. They were very old school. They had no fancy freezers, for example, to keep the guests' fish cold. Instead, all the fish were kept under the dock, in a special, submerged box accessed by a trap door near the cleaning table. The scale they weighed the fish on was another one of those balance beams, like the one Troutbreath used at Big Bay. They kept it polished, the weights clean and shining. They took weigh-ins very seriously. For a fish to be called a tyee, it had to be exactly thirty pounds and not an ounce less.

The big whirlpools and upwellings might be a concern, even life-threatening, but they were nothing compared to a look of disappointment from Lyle Donovan. With his big fish headed right for me, I had no time to reel my line in before I got out of his way. I reached down for my knife again.

Five minutes later, I was tied up at the small dock, again. The two boats were still there but getting ready to leave. I started the whole process again.

But I was getting a little concerned. I only had one more six-ounce weight with me; the eights and tens might be too heavy to find the coho sweet spot. I paid even more attention to getting my rod strung up again. With all the excitement in the fishing holes, it was easy to get distracted and tie a bad knot or miss stringing an eye up the rod. I took my time finding just the right small herring and again cut it at an angle I knew would improve the spin that the coho liked. I untied from the small float once more and drifted out into the back eddy, looking for a spot.

When I finally took up a position, Heidi was a little ahead of me, with two clients, in the carousel of boats. I was not surprised to see the rod on her port side and closest to me suddenly start bouncing out of her client's hands.

She yelled, "Reel! Stand up and reel. Reel as hard as you can!"

Her voice cut through the rumble of the rapids, the shrill whine of my engine as I tried backing up, and the cries coming from the other boats. Her client was a tad slow to stand up and start reeling his line. He looked at her blankly. His lips moved, but he couldn't form any words. I recognized the look. The man was frozen in place.

A lovely, big northern coho flew out of the water, headed toward Heidi's boat. It appeared again, a little closer to them this time. I knew it was on Heidi's line long before her customer believed what she was trying to tell him.

I spun my boat around to head back up the current. It was the only place available to get out of their way. Having just one line in the water gave me much more manoeuvrability. I was at a right angle to Heidi's boat, trying to motor past them, when the coho flew out of the water again. This time it smacked her client on the side of his face. As the fish disappeared back into the water, the client turned to look at Heidi. His baseball hat was knocked sideways, and the whole side of his face dripped with salmon slime mixed with shimmering fish scales.

"Ow! Heidi!" the man wailed, taking his eyes off the rod to look at Heidi. "You didn't have to slap me that hard! I stood up and I'm reeling as fast as I can!"

The man still had no clue that the beautiful northern, now clearing the water on the other side of their boat, was attached to his line. His partner in the seat beside him did his best to explain it.

"You idiot!" he yelled. "Heidi didn't slap you—it was the goddamn fish! Now, reel!"

As I tried to continue my manoeuvre to get out of their way, my rod started to bounce in my hands. Then suddenly, as if I had hooked on to a passing bullet train, the tip of my rod plunged into the water and the line started screaming off the reel. I knew instantly that this was no coho.

The rod tip plunged deep into the current swirling past me. I could feel the power of the fish. The line ran under my boat, so I gunned my motor and spun away from it. I had to keep my boat upstream from the direction the salmon was taking.

Heidi, despite all the chaos on her boat, saw what had just happened and made room for me.

"Holy shit!" Heidi's eyes were wide as we swooped past each other.

I really needed to get away from all the boats. The salmon was already heading from the centre of the Second Hole out to the open water of Cordero Channel. I took a moment to look around. Three more boats were headed down the tide toward me. The bullet train I was holding in my hands was already far out in front. I had to follow, but exiting the Second Hole at this spot was something of a problem.

Between me and the main channel was the chain of whirlpools. They began at the First Hole and by the time they arrived where I was now heading, they had grown huge, opening out completely. Right beside me was one about sixty feet across, with another one the same size in the chain right behind it.

Everything had happened so quickly that I hadn't even started my big motor. Now was a good time. I turned the key, and mercifully the big engine roared to life. I quickly stopped the little engine and pulled it up out of the way with one hand while I kept playing the salmon with the other. Then, with the big motor running now, I took its tiller arm and turned the boat, aiming between the two whirlpools.

The whirlpools spun opposite to the Second Hole back eddy. My bow was already pointed in the right direction, and I eased farther out, feeling myself being caught by their push. I was riding the surge, using my boat as a surfboard. Luckily, I had judged correctly. I felt my boat lift. I was now up in the air with the whirlpools on either side, riding the pressure ridge between them as the main current swept my boat and the whirlpools before it.

I looked down into the two gaping maws on either side. Large chunks of driftwood, sea foam, and whole pieces of kelp and other assorted debris churned inside them. It was like being between two gigantic boiling cauldrons; the mist thrown up by the action of the water was the steam rising from them.

A few moments before, I had been peacefully drifting in a kelp bed. A very short time later, and here I was playing a big fish out of the Second Hole.

It was better not to overthink my situation.

The sound of the water took me over, beyond sound. It entered my body; I felt rather than heard it. The power of the water thrummed in my chest. No matter how much you might prepare yourself for such an experience, how much you might want it, nothing can prepare you for the reality. The first time you experience this, it might cause some panic. Then, as you get more comfortable among the whirlpools, you start to enjoy it. You begin to seek it out. If you are away from it for any length of time, you miss it.

By now, my line was high out of the water, which dripped off the line like pearls on a string. The fish was seventy feet away on the other side of the whirlpool, down the current from me. I drove my boat across the pressure ridge out into the main channel. With one hand still holding the rod and the other steering the boat, it was impossible to reel in any line. Once again, I turned the boat upstream and drove away from the fish. I let the fish run and used the direction of the boat to keep the line tight. I blocked the driftwood and debris that followed me using the hull of the boat.

Both the fish and I were being pushed by the tide. The whirlpools began to flatten out; the water was still in turmoil, but less dangerous. I could let the engine idle while I retrieved as much line as possible. I had almost caught up to the salmon when my line went tight, and the rod bent over into the water. The fish was taking one more desperate run.

It was heading for Kelsey Point, the point of land that protected the Stuart Island Resort from the worst of the tide. A huge field of debris waited for me there—logs, balls of kelp, branches—all caught in the tide line and impossible to pass through safely.

I pulled up on the rod and tried to gather more line. I hauled up carefully, then dropped the rod tip, reeling in foot by foot. Over and over, I dropped the rod and reeled in the line. I could feel the salmon shaking its head, trying to spit out the hook. Just before Kelsey Point, by the cove called Machine Shop Bay, the salmon took another shorter run and headed into it.

It went deep this time, and there it skulked. I kept the line tight, the rod bent right over, with as much pull as I dared. One of the guides went by, returning to the Second Hole after playing their own fish down the tide.

"Come on, get that little thing in the boat!" he yelled as he slowed down to pass me carefully. His two customers stared; they were the most I was going to get for spectators.

The struggle continued. The salmon and I had drifted right into Machine Shop Bay, where the water was shallower, the current not as strong. It was the best place to finish this battle. I kept trying to retrieve the line, pulling up the rod and reeling in as much as the fish let me. Slowly, I gained on it.

Finally, I saw the salmon under the water. When you see a salmon come up like that for a client, they look big. Because it was on my line, because this time I was the client, I was sure it was the biggest one I had ever seen.

Keeping the line taut, I carefully reached down and picked up my landing net. I got the fish turning toward me. When my weight was at the tip of the rod, I strained to lift it as high as I could with my left arm. I let the net slip through my other hand until I was holding it at the very end of the handle. I waited. As the fish swam in a circle, I watched and waited a moment longer. The timing had to be just right.

The fish was tired after the long fight. It rolled over onto its side. When its circling brought it nearest to me, I dropped the landing net in front of it, letting the mesh open in the current. The fish swam into it. I dropped the rod onto the floor of the boat and pulled back on the net. As the mesh closed over the fish, I reached down with the hand that had just been holding the rod and grabbed the hoop of the landing net. With one heave, the salmon was on the floor of my boat.

I quickly used my fish bonker to put the salmon down. I had too much respect for this magnificent creature to let it suffer. Then I sat down and took in what had just happened. I needed to catch my breath and let the shaking of my hands subside. At the bottom of my boat lay a sleek chinook salmon, glistening silver in the sun. It reached almost from one side of my boat to the other. I was sure it was a tyee, but it seemed too athletic to be of the requisite weight. While it looked huge in the water, a more sober inspection suggested I get it weighed as quickly as possible. The late summer sun was still hot enough to make it lose a pound or so.

The Stuart Island Resort was a short distance away. Jamie, the owner, was on the dock and saw me struggle out of the boat. I was only too happy to have him grab the other side of the gills. We had it up on the scales in a moment. When the arm of the scale finally settled, the salmon weighed thirty-one-and-a-half pounds.

I really had landed a tyee out of the Second Hole.

I knew Jamie well. He gave out bronze lapel pins, a leaping salmon with SIR stamped at the bottom, to clients who caught a tyee. For a fish over forty pounds, the fish's eye was a diamond chip. For a fish over fifty, the eye was a ruby. With this fish safely on the scales, he told me to come with him to the office. With some ceremony, he gave me one of his bronze tyee pins.

That lox was very good—and there was so much of it. But it is all long finished by now. That little trophy, though, hardly bigger than a nickel, is still one of my prized possessions.

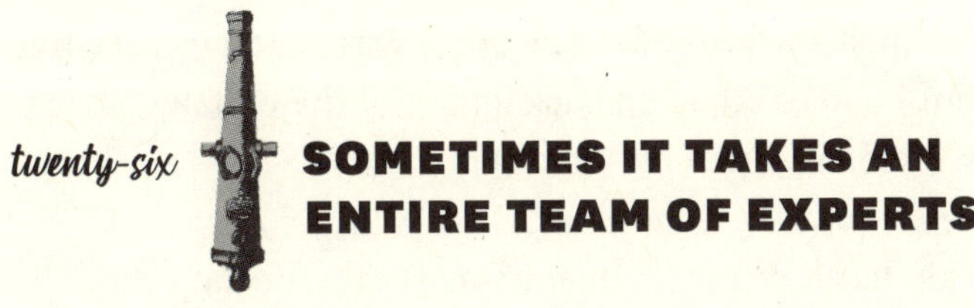

twenty-six SOMETIMES IT TAKES AN ENTIRE TEAM OF EXPERTS

I WAS WALKING past the fantail of the Brelands' classic yacht when a familiar voice called down to me.

"Hey, Dave, I hear you caught a nice one in Second Hole!" I looked up into the smiling face of Wet Lenny. He motioned for me to join him. "Let me get you a beer or something."

At this point in my career as a guide, I was beginning to understand the limits of my control. I really was just a plaything for the fishing gods. If I was supposed to be swallowed by a whirlpool, I didn't have to worry about it. If Lucky Petersen and I shared the same problem after talking with Wet Lenny? I accepted I wasn't going to catch a fish for the next three days. I wasn't going to be rude and not speak to him. After all, I was curious to hear what he had been doing. That knowledge would, no doubt, be worth three days of getting skunked.

The fantail of the Brelands' classic yacht was perfectly designed to provide comfortable seating and almost any beverage of choice. It was like the bar car on the Orient Express. Wet Lenny bustled about, and in short order I was seated and within reach of a cold beer.

"So, here is to a tyee out the Second Hole." Wet Lenny clinked my glass. "Tell me all about it."

"There isn't much to tell, really."

"How deep were you?"

"I had just started to let line out. I was at about forty-five feet, but I had to stop and back up out of the way. I was right beside Heidi playing a big coho."

"Were you using a cut-plug?"

"Yeah, but just a little one. I was set up for the coho. The cut-plug had the top hook just in the cavity." I made a gesture with my hand, the universal top hook gesture, showing how you place the hook into the backbone of your herring. "You know, to give it a faster spin. I mean, when those coho are hungry, you could catch one with the pop top from a can of beer! I must have backed right on top of the tyee and hit it on the nose."

"You think it was just pure luck?"

"Mostly that. And knowing when to get out of people's way."

"You seem to do be able to do that with annoying frequency."

"What, get out of people's way?"

"No, hit big fish on the nose with your bait. Didn't you catch a tyee for Morris Goldfarb the same way?"

"You have a long memory, my friend, a very long memory. I do try to get out of my own way as much as possible. You know, let the fish gods indulge their sense of humour."

This was something I knew Wet Lenny was all too familiar with.

"What have you been up to, though? I didn't see you up here at all last summer." I wanted to change the subject.

"Mr. Breland and I were helping establish an association," said Wet Lenny. "We think it's going to be a very important development for the preservation of wild salmon."

"How is that?"

"If things work out the way we are expecting, it will give the wild salmon a chance to rest and replenish their numbers. People are beginning to realize the stocks are getting depleted. Did you hear the Sun Free Salmon Derby isn't going to happen anymore?"

"No, I hadn't heard that. That derby is famous! It's been going for years."

"Since 1940, to be exact. Last summer was the final year."

"Wow, that says a lot. So, what are you going to do? Are you sharing your expertise?"

"Me? No, Mr. Breland is developing an entire team of experts. They will support the work of the association we are going to put in place. It's going to implement a method that will replace wild salmon for the commercial market with an abundant alternative."

"Oh yeah? What method is that? And what alternative is there?"

Wet Lenny smiled. It wasn't a triumphant smile; it was quite humble, in its way. It was the smile of a man who had found his true calling. He paused and said, "Fish farming!"

twenty-seven ANCIENT HISTORY

THE PILE OF life jackets in the shed on Troutbreath's dock was a remnant of the past. The old red and orange kapok-filled vests were rarely used for their intended purpose as the new survival suits grew in popularity—and for good reason. You might look like a giant banana, but your chances of surviving the frigid water were greatly improved. But these aptly named suits didn't make very comfortable seating covers. The small luxury of sitting on a lifejacket in a boat shed would one day soon disappear.

Troutbreath, Lawrence, and I were arranged on these artifacts as comfort dictated, having one of those end-of-season chats that touched on everything and landed on nothing. Earlier in the day, Troutbreath had sent a couple of rookies off to find some firewood. A few guides remained, trying to get every possible hour on the water.

Rain was in the forecast. The old shack could be very damp.

The rookies returned noisily. They seemed quite excited about something they had found.

"Hey, Troutbreath, you gotta see this!" They marched right up to the front of the shack, one of them carrying an obviously heavy canvas bag.

Troutbreath roused himself slowly off his kapok seat. Excited rookies were a common phenomenon. It usually didn't take much to get them going.

"You won't believe what we found. You gotta see it!"

Troutbreath did his best to look noncommittal. He wasn't going to let himself get swept up by rookie excitement.

The guy carrying the sack put it down and reached into it with both hands. With some trouble, he lifted out a rusted metal ball. At first glance, it looked like one of those downrigger weights the commercial trollers used, although those were usually made of lead that didn't rust.

Troutbreath seemed in awe of the ball. He asked in a quiet voice, "Where did you get that?"

"Well, you sent us off to find firewood. There was an old dead snag at the south end of the island. You know, it's in behind that little cliff. When we cut into the trunk of the tree, the chainsaw dinged it. There were sparks and everything. You can see the mark left by the chain."

He pointed at a bright little scar in the rust, as if we might not believe them.

"Is it what we think it is?"

"And what, exactly, do you think it is?" asked Troutbreath mildly. I could see he was suppressing some excitement of his own.

"Buried in the tree like that, we're thinking it's a cannonball. It's probably what killed the tree in the first place. But I mean, this thing has got to be ancient. How did it even get there?"

Troutbreath was rubbing a spot on his chest. I had noticed him sporting a nasty bruise not even a couple of weeks ago; no doubt some purple and yellow splotches remained.

"Put it back in the bag and hand it to me. I want to try something."

The guide did as he was told and handed the package across the narrow counter. Troutbreath stepped outside with it and walked over to the fish scale. He hung the bag off the hook and made some adjustments until it came to rest.

"There you go, it weighs about four pounds. As far as I know, the only ship capable of shooting a ball of iron like that into a tree was Vancouver's ship *Discovery*. They were armed with ten four-pounder cannons."

"Woah! That's way too cool!"

"That was, what..." said the more thoughtful one of the two. "Like, hundreds of years ago or something? This thing really is old!"

Unknown to any of us, Troutbreath was in shock. He was only too familiar with this cannonball. It might be ancient history to these two guys, but it was recent enough for him. Troutbreath still had the marks from his encounter with the tree root. He did the best he could to look calm and detached.

"That's so cool! It's a piece of history, man! When were those guys here?"

"If I remember correctly, they were here in 1792, so that's... 193 years, not quite two centuries." We all respected Troutbreath's mathematical abilities—it was what he did most of the summer, after all.

"Well, that's awesome! If it really is that old, it's ancient history."

"What are you going to do with it? It would look great on the shelf there," I said.

Troutbreath had kind of a trophy shelf built on the wall behind the service counter.

"Sure, put it on display," one rookie said. "No one will believe us. We might have found it, but until they hear it from you, no one will take us seriously."

"Yeah," the other confirmed. "I mean, look at us." They were covered in sawdust. "I wouldn't take us seriously either."

"We gotta go empty the firewood out of the boat anyway." They both turned toward the heavily laden guide boat behind them.

After they left, the three of us took turns hefting the four-pound cannonball.

twenty-eight

NOW THAT YOU MENTION IT

WHEN IT WAS Lawrence's turn, he sat down with the cannonball, quietly holding it in his arms like a rare and precious object.

"It's almost like holding a sacred stone," he said after a time. "Like a seer stone, eh?"

Troutbreath went back to absently holding his injured chest.

"What's a seer stone? If you don't mind me asking," I said.

"It's kind of a living thing, in Indigenous cultures," Lawrence explained. "It has its own power, a life and a spirit. It exists independently. No one owns it; it exists for everyone and can be revered by all the tribes. It has the power to bring people together. Maybe the most well-known one is the Manitou Stone, which legend says was originally located somewhere in the northern plains of Alberta. They think it's a meteorite. An object from the stars. Some missionary named McDougall stole it back in 1866. Things kind of took a turn for the worse after that. I'd guess you can feel it too."

Troutbreath listened, then looked down at his hand rubbing his chest. As much as he wanted to say something about his own special connection to those four pounds of cast iron, he had made some promises. He was bound by those promises; Lars and Gunnar had taken some risks confiding in him.

He removed his hand and asked Lawrence, "What makes you say that I can feel it??"

"Where are your folks from?"

"You mean my parents?" Troutbreath looked at him curiously. He had never asked himself many questions about his background.

"I'm just wondering," said Lawrence.

"I don't know where my biological parents were from. I was adopted young, and my parents were, you know, always my parents. I've never looked for my real parents. I guess I've never thought about it much."

"How old are you?"

"Twenty-six," Troutbreath answered.

"Wow, you seem so much older than that."

"Yeah, I get that all the time," Troutbreath sighed.

"So, you were born in fifty-nine. That was a couple of years before it really got started. You ever think you could have been a part of what they call the 'Sixties Scoop'?"

"Calling it the 'Sixties Scoop' makes it sound like a trip to the ice cream parlour. Wasn't that First Nations kids, though?"

"Well, you ever get the feeling you might be out of a different time and place than everyone else? Like, time moves differently for you? Things tend to lurch out of your control without warning?"

Troutbreath grinned sheepishly; at that moment he felt completely transparent. He had always honoured his promise to Lars and Gunnar. He had never told anyone what they were able to do. Who would believe it, anyway? But somehow, it seemed Lawrence knew something.

"Well, maybe sometimes?"

"Would you rather make a trade for something than pay actual money for it?"

"What are you saying?"

"You ever think you might be First Nations?"

Troutbreath froze. You could almost hear the pieces falling into place.

"You think that's possible?"

"Are you kidding? Do you know how many people ask me if I'm your brother? I think it is entirely possible."

"What do you think, Dave?" Troutbreath said, looking right at me.

"Aw, man, it's not like I'm any kind of authority."

"I trust your opinion, though; you pay attention and don't miss much. You can say what you think."

"Well, you know," I said, knowing I had permission. "Now that you mention it."

twenty-nine BRAVO ALPHA BRAVO YANKEE

"HELLO? HELLO... MUM?"

"Yes."

"Mum?"

"I'm still here."

"I love you, Mum."

"Oh, that's nice."

"Mum? Can you hear me, Mum?"

"Yes. I can hear you."

"Hello, Mum?"

"Yes."

"I love you, Mum."

The conversation had been going on like this for some time now. Some very drunk-sounding guy was having a conversation of sorts with his elderly and very patient mother on the radio telephone. Vop was next in line for the marine operator. He had to listen in on the line to know when they were finished. So far, Vop had been standing by for a good twenty minutes.

"Mum. Hello, Mum?"

"Yes."

"I love you, Mum."

"That's nice, dear."

It was riveting stuff. As he waited, Vop's anxiety grew. His imagination began to take over. He had stopped in to fill up his gas tanks and Troutbreath had passed along a message to call Carol at home on Cortes. It sounded urgent, and the longer he had to wait his turn, the more urgent it seemed.

"Mum? Can you hear me, Mum?"

Vop was pretty sure this question had been asked and answered. Still, calling out from Stuart Island using the ship-to-shore radio telephone was not easy. There were only a small number of available channels. Once you got on, you had to talk with the marine operator, who would dial the land line number for you and then put it through on that radio channel. Once you were in the queue, it was best to wait your turn.

"Mum. I love you, Mum."

Vop was beginning to give up. He kept waiting only because it was so unusual for Carol to get in touch this way.

Finally, there was a long pause and then the line went dead. The clipped clinical voice of the female marine operator cut in.

"Big Bay, Big Bay, are you still standing by? Over."

Vop almost missed his moment. He managed to blurt out, "Yes, that's me. I'm Big Boy, uh, Bay. Still standing by. Um, over."

"What is the name and number of the party you wish to contact?"

Vop gave the number of the neighbour's line, where he knew Carol was waiting. He listened to the sound of dialing and then a phone ringing. Carol picked up quickly.

"I have a call from Big Bay for a Carol. Are you willing to accept the charges? Over."

The marine operator was clear and emotionless. She needed a land line to apply the connection charges. Vop heard Carol's familiar voice as she accepted the call. The operator thanked her and let her know the line was now open. Carol tried to speak, but all Vop heard was the crackle of static.

"Vop? Can you … me … Um, over?"

"Say that again, Carol. You're breaking up pretty bad at this end … Um, over."

"Okay, can …"

"No, it's getting worse. Try giving it a minute, then speak."

"How about now? I have some important news to tell you. I saw the doc …"

"I had you there for a second, but now you're gone again. Can you hear me? Over."

"I got the … results … and w…"

"Try talking slower," Vop offered helpfully.

"Aw, Honey, that … nev … anything … prob …"

"No, lost you again. What is you want to tell me? Over."

"We are having a bab …"

"A bab? You mean like a barbecue? Over."

"No, a ba … Oh … this is impo … You are ha … a Bravo Alpha Bravo Yankee. Over."

"I love you too, baby, but maybe we should try this again when the reception is better? Over!" By now, Vop was yelling into the microphone, so everyone in the store could hear him. This loud exchange of feelings was making him uncomfortable.

"I'll try calling again maybe tomorrow. Over!"

When Vop got back to the house later, I asked him what was so important. Why did Carol want to subject herself to a radio telephone call?

"I don't really know. The connection was terrible. I think she was just lonely, you know. She kept trying to call me her babe. Ended up spelling it out, Bravo-Alpha-Bravo-Yankee."

"Really? You think she was trying to tell you something you already know? I mean, B-A-B-Y—you know what that spells?"

Vop's eyes suddenly widened. There was a pause as the penny started to drop. The penny dropped for a very long time before it finally found somewhere to land.

"Holy shit!"

Vop turned and ran toward the door. "I've got to go make another phone call!" he yelled at me over his shoulder.

thirty ONE LAST TIDE

THE OLD MAN let his boat get pushed back to the top of the Second Hole once more. He watched carefully along the shore, looking for his markers, tracking his position, triangulating it precisely. At just the right moment, he turned the bow of the boat out. The hull would catch the current and ride it along the outside to complete the circle around the hole. On the downward path, using the same method but before he got too close to the reef, he turned the bow toward the shore. He could catch the back eddy that took him back to the top of the hole again, the endless circuit.

One more, just one more drift. If you had bait in the water, there was always that chance. The man watched the shore and, as he drifted over the rocks and crevices hidden in the water below, he counted. His lips moved endlessly as he reeled the line up over a rock or tried to find the entrance to the right crevice where the big one might be lurking.

Sometimes he put the rod in the holder and watched the tip, looking for that telltale bounce. Nothing takes the bait quite like a big salmon. As he concentrated on even the slightest movement, he absently kneaded the palm of his left hand. He had been in the doctor's office again. As the doctor removed more of his sun-damaged skin, freezing it off with liquid nitrogen, he cited more warnings. The old man was only too aware of the dangers. He was beginning to look like a hard wax model of himself, an effigy that had been left in the sun too long and was beginning to melt.

He circled endlessly, looking, hoping for the next big fish, the next bragging rights, the next chance to feel that rush of excitement. Perhaps this would be the time. This would be the moment that gave it all some kind of meaning. His lips moved endlessly, as he spelled out his desires, his needs, looking for the end of his search. But by now, the search was beyond that kind of revelation; by now, it was purely the search itself.

Even this late in the season, the sun was still hot. He wore a wide-brimmed hat with a piece of cloth hanging down to cover the sides and back of his neck. He wore another piece of cloth over his shoulders like a cape. The light fabric was almost see-through. It looked like old gauzy curtains with a pale blue floral pattern, perhaps something he had found in the bottom of a seldom-visited drawer. He wore white gloves on his hands, and his lips and nose were white from the zinc oxide he had applied. He was a white and pale-blue shadow of himself, a revenant.

His boat rose and fell on the greasy swells. The rod holder made a metallic creak as it moved. Not a breath of air disturbed the surface of the water. The motion of the boat drifting along made the gauzy coverings flap lazily against his body, like the tattered sails of a ghost ship, trying to summon the wind.

EPILOGUE

THE BRITISH COLUMBIA Salmon Farmers Association was formed in 1984. I did the best I could in this trilogy to ignore the obvious coincidences regarding the date. At that time, there was hope that using farmed salmon for commercial purposes would give the wild salmon a "rest." The idea was adopted quite rapidly. From time to time, I still get asked for my thoughts regarding the fish farms' worth and effectiveness. The question always prompts the following story.

Some four or five years after the formation of the association, I was working as a resident guide at the Stuart Island Resort. By then, a fish farm was already established up in Ramsay Arm. At the beginning of that summer's guiding season, the mail plane, which could only use the government dock at the resort for passenger drop-off or pick-up, delivered a rather bewildered-looking young guy carrying a duffle bag. One of the perks of my job was getting to talk with random strangers that appeared at the resort complex.

It turned out he was trying to get to the fish farm at Ramsay Arm. He was told, of course, that the mail plane was only allowed to pick up and drop off passengers at a designated government dock. There was little to no other explanation or suggestion of how he was supposed to get the rest of the way to his final destination. The best the pilot could do was to drop him off at Stuart Island with the hope of finding a boat to take him the rest of the way.

Going on unplanned trips up the Arm was another one of the perks of my job. The scenery is quite spectacular. Also, the look of relief on the poor guy's face, after I told him to hop in my guide boat and I would take him there, was worth the gas money.

Ramsay Arm is just south of Stuart Island. You hang a left just past New Church House. The fish farm was in a small, protected bay close to the entrance across from Raza Island. It didn't take us long to get there. As I got closer to the complex of docks, I could see two men on the one nearest to us, the dock I was already heading towards. One guy stood leaning over watching as the other guy, on his stomach, waved something in his hand at whatever was under the dock.

The dock sat quite high out of the water and gave me, in my low guide boat, a good view under it. I caught a glimpse of a big sea otter disappearing under the water. The two guys were so caught up in what they were doing, they didn't even notice us pull up a short distance from their dock.

"Oh, goddamn it, he's gone again, and this damn thing isn't working!" the guy on his stomach wailed.

He stood up and I could see the "damn thing" he had in his hand was a small semi-automatic pistol. He whacked at it a couple of times with his other hand, making guttural sounds of exasperation as he did so.

"Have you tried jiggling the safety? Maybe the salty sea air is making it stick," the other guy offered helpfully. They still gave us no notice at all.

"No, goddamn it, I've jiggled it enough times already. It isn't the safety. The cocking lever must not be engaging properly." The man started pulling at the slide on top of the gun, cursing all the time. He mentioned more than once how much money they had spent on a device that didn't work.

Meanwhile, the young, bewildered guy and I floated just a few feet away. Neither of us wanted to startle the man with the gun, whether it was working properly or not. So, we both sat quietly, my engine idling, and watched the scene unfolding before us.

I heard the slight sound of water. Looking under the dock I could see the otter had resurfaced. He turned to me; he obviously knew we had pulled into the dock, but he didn't seem the least bit concerned. Perhaps he sensed we were harmless.

The otter was enjoying himself. Apparently this had been playing out for some time before we got there. I got the impression the otter was a regular here, and who could blame him? The little bay was home to several large net pens, each of them about the size of an Olympic swimming pool. They held captive the Arctic salmon that were becoming the otter's favourite food. There was always going to be the odd escapee here and there.

When it came to taking care of the wild salmon, the people who took it upon themselves to make decisions about their management now were basically the same people who thought Old Church House Bay would be a fine location for a village. The system Indigenous Peoples had to manage and harvest salmon had served very well for generations. Captain Vancouver was so taken by the results—by the number and size of salmon in the water—he thought to mention it in his logbook. Even in the dry, official naval record, you get a sense of Vancouver's awe. However, no one bothered to ask Indigenous Peoples for their advice on salmon enhancement. By the 1920s, sixty- or seventy-pound spring salmon returning to the rivers were still not uncommon. But unfortunately, for so many different reasons, the decline had already set in.

The completion of the national railway through the Fraser Canyon, for example, caused landslides that effectively blocked the Fraser River. That river had hosted the largest run of salmon in the world, and just like that, it was cut off. Between landslides and spawning beds being clogged with sawdust, clear-cut logging stripping away shade trees, and toxic mine waste being released in places like Howe Sound, where I grew up, less than two hundred years after the voyage of Vancouver, the spring salmon have been reduced to ten percent of their pre-contact numbers. Looking at the two characters arguing above us on the fish farm float—two guys in charge of giving the wildlife "a rest"—I was once again reminded of why there was an Old Church House and a New Church House.

The otter nodded towards me, as if he was pleased to have witnesses. Otters were, after all, a protected species, almost driven to extinction by the Russian fur trade. He flashed a human-like smile and—I swear I am not exaggerating—gave me the universal *what the hell is wrong with these people* look. Then he disappeared under the water one more time, making good his escape.

ACKNOWLEDGEMENTS

I WOULD LIKE to acknowledge Kerriann for her patient support and encouragement.

I gratefully acknowledge the Nuxalk Peoples, also known as the Bella Coola, the ləkʷəŋən (Lekwungen) Peoples, and all the Coast Salish Peoples who have so many more stories to be told.

Also, a big thank-you to Daphne, Program Coordinator at the Cowichan Bay Maritime Centre.

ABOUT THE AUTHOR

DAVID GIBLIN is a visual artist and writer who worked for fifteen years as a salmon fishing guide on Stuart Island, roughly forty miles east of central Vancouver Island. This experience provided a fertile environment for the incubation of great fishing stories, and eventually led to the publication of *The Codfish Dream* and *Gilly the Ghillie*, the first two books in Giblin's West Coast Fishing Guide trilogy.

KERRIANN CARDINAL is a film producer, actor, and storyteller of Métis descent. She has worked on numerous movies and TV series, including the feature film and limited series productions of *Bones of Crows*.

Go back to the beginning of the West Coast Fishing Guide trilogy...

THE CODFISH DREAM

Chronicles of a West Coast Fishing Guide

ISBN 978-1-77203-242-0 (paperback)
ISBN 978-1-77203-243-7 (e-book)

"You'll meet eccentric shore workers, wealthy guests who arrive by yacht and floatplane, as well as essential guides Big Jake, Lucky Petersen, Vop and Wet Lenny... A deadpan narrative keeps the absurdity coming as earnest RCMP, FBI and Fisheries officers encounter the salmon-obsessed denizens of the island resort. This book is a keeper."

WESTERN MARINER

"David Giblin is a marvellous storyteller, and *The Codfish Dream* is a wonderful book: witty, whimsical, well-written, and a terrific read from cover to cover."

IAN FERGUSON, author of the Stephen Leacock Medal-winning *Village of the Small Houses* and *The Survival Guide to British Columbia*

A colourful portrait of life in a fishing village on the BC coast.

The first book collecting a series of hilarious, strange, keenly observed, true (or mostly true) stories of David Giblin's experiences as a fishing guide on the BC coast. These whimisical tales are held together by a thread of international intrigue that affects everyone in the small community of Stuart Island over one eventful summer, when FBI agents visit the island to investigate insider trading. *The Codfish Dream* is an unforgettable book imbued with an undeniable sense of place and time.

The adventures continue . . .

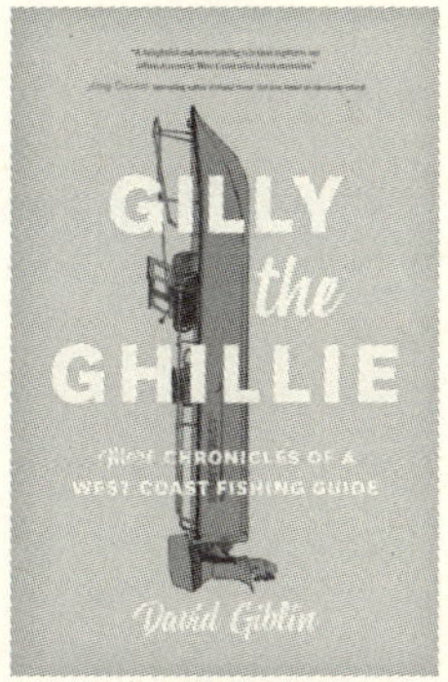

GILLY THE GHILLIE

More Chronicles of a West Coast Fishing Guide

ISBN 978-1-77203-335-9 (paperback)
ISBN 978-1-77203-336-6 (e-book)

"A delightful and entertaining tale which captures our (often eccentric) West Coast Island communities complete with gum boots, pot plants, fish gutting, wood stoves and salty blustery storms. Makes me want to get a fishing guide and go fishing!"
ANNY SCOONES, bestselling author of *Island Home: Out and About on Vancouver Island*

"A winningly entertaining set of linked stories concerning the lives of fishing guides and their clients along the upper BC coast. The foibles of characters such as Baba, Troutbreath, and the eponymous Gilly, along with the author's understated dry humour, beg the question—what will they get up to next?"
DON HUNTER, author of the Leacock Award-shortlisted *Spinner's Inlet* and *Return to Spinner's Inlet*

Tall tales of coastal adventures, colourful locals, privileged tourists, and elusive fish abound in this hilariously offbeat sequel to *The Codfish Dream*.

David Giblin returns with more hilarious and bizarre stories that reveal as much about the quirkiness of small coastal communities as they do about human nature itself. Now, in his second book of short interconnected stories set in the 1980s, Giblin introduces us to Gilly, the first female fishing guide to grace the tiny island, whose mere presence is enough to shake the foundations of the very insular, all-male guiding community. With the return of delightfully eccentric characters including VOP, Troutbreath, Lucky Peterson, and Wet Lenny, this rollicking maritime adventure will appeal to anyone who ever gutted a fish and lived to tell the tale.